Wilkinson Waldorf Curriculum
Series

TEACHING HISTORY

Volume I

Ancient Civilizations

Greece and Rome

Roy Wilkinson

RSCP

The publisher is grateful for the encouragement and support of Robert Dulaney in making this new edition possible.

The name Waldorf really belongs only to the first school of its type, the one founded by Rudolf Steiner in Stuttgart, Germany for the children of the workers at the Waldorf-Astoria factory. It has since been adopted as the generic name of schools conducted according to Rudolf Steiner's recommendations. In place of Waldorf some establishments call themselves Rudolf Steiner schools. Others take a distinctive name and add Waldorf or Rudolf Steiner in some connection as a subtitle.

These notes, revised from the original version published in 1973, are intended for the use of teachers, parents, and all those interested in the education of the child. They are based on the author's life-long contact with Rudolf Steiner's work, including thirty years practical experience in the classroom.

Revised 2000

ISBN 0-945803-44-3

Book orders may be made through Rudolf Steiner College Bookstore. Tel. 916-961-8729, FAX 916-961-3032.

Rudolf Steiner College Press
9200 Fair Oaks Blvd.
Fair Oaks, CA. 95628 U.S.A.

The Ancient Civilizations

INTRODUCTION

The panorama of history is so wide that the teacher may well despair before ever he gets started. History comprises all that has happened from the beginning of time, at whatever point we may set that, to the present. It is an enormous span, and the mind boggles at the thought of trying to encompass it, let alone digest it and represent it to children at school. Since it is obviously impossible to cover the whole field, we must narrow it to essentials; but before embarking on the actual teaching of the subject, we might try to clarify our minds as to what it really is.

In the ordinary school sense, history is a sequence of events about which one learns in chronological order. It is usual to devote a great deal of time to national history and, for examination purposes, to study a set period. Neither of these is particularly educative. Let us therefore seek a more exact definition. History is the story of the development of humanity, but as humanity is made up of individuals, history is also the story of people. The human being himself goes through an evolution, and here we are not thinking in the Darwinian sense, but in the sense of a development of the mind. The modern human mind works in a certain way. In ancient times it was different. It is this change in the state of the mind which brings about the external changes, i.e., the scenes or phenomena of history. History is not merely a sequence of events. The sequences are dependent on the evolution of the mind. That is to say: history is not something which only takes place on the physical plane. The events are the manifestations of spiritual impulses which arise within the human soul. It is feasible to think of such impulses being given by superhuman agencies. One has only to think of the inspiration given to the founders of the great religions, to the prophets of the Old Testament, or to consider the voices heard by Joan of Arc. That there can be negative influences is also fairly obvious. We have experienced madmen like Caligula. In more recent times one might even think of a Hitler as being influenced or possessed by demonic beings.

What is this change that has taken place? We can look upon the evolution of the human being as a development of individuality, as a development of ego-consciousness, and along with this there goes a deeper penetration into the physical world. We can see a parallel to this in the growth of the individual.

Small children live in a dream-like state and are directed by the more mature adults. In the course of time they become independent, conscious of themselves as individuals, aware of their own Ego, and they learn to cope with the material world. In early civilizations the mass of the people lived in a child-like state and were guided and directed by personalities who in some respects were more mature, i.e., their priests and kings. These, in turn, were guided by spiritual beings—gods—and were what is known as "initiates," by which is meant that they had direct experience of a supersensible world. Their knowledge and the faculties to obtain such knowledge were cultivated in the so-called Mysteries or Mystery Schools, the equivalent of what today would be the theological college. As far as the ordinary human being is concerned, the development has been from a state of dream-like dependence to the self-reliant self-consciousness of today.

The change, of course, does not reveal itself uniformly over the whole world. When we speak of the evolution of the human being in the above sense, we look to the post-Atlantean cultural epochs as described by Dr. Steiner, where we can trace the development. These are: Ancient India, Ancient Persia or Iran, Egypt/Babylonia, Greece/Rome, Europe, which occurred in historical sequence.

Of course there were other peoples living in different parts of the world with other cultures and other ways of living but this is a sepatate study and can be dealt with in other contexts such as the Geography lessons. It is important for children to have, eventually, a relationship to the wonderful variety of humanity and to appreciate the various gifts and characteristics of every people.

By way of example to show how the state of mind or consciousness has changed, one has only to consider Greek times and the beginning of philosophy. One might pose the question: why did philosophy begin about the year 600 BC? The answer is that the Greeks were the first people in the world to *think* in the way we now understand the word. There were earlier periods in the course of human development when human beings did not experience thought in the way they do today. They experienced pictures or images and the legacy of these pictures is to be found in the mythologies. A change comes about in 600 BC with the Greek philosophers who first feel that the soul is something separate from nature. Up to that time, people had felt that something causes thunder, furthers plant growth, moves the hand, etc., but now there came the realization of a difference between outer and inner happenings. The soul was experienced as something separate from the rest of the world, as an independent entity. As a corollary, the question naturally arose as to the soul's origin. It was felt that basically the soul belonged to the good powers, but was surrounded by an imperfect world. To find the primeval Good, it had to trace its way back to its origins. To do this, it must experience its former incarnations. It was this belief which led to the Pythagorean teaching of the wandering of the soul.

Many of the philosophers of this period show how inner and outer life are not yet freed from one another, and they struggle with the problem of differentiating between what is outer spiritual vision and what is inner process. A definite stage is reached with Socrates who finds that the wisdom which had been given in the Mysteries, as direct experience, can be found in the soul by means of thought. He it is who teaches to trust in thought. For this reason, he was considered to be betraying the mysteries and corrupting the youth. Thus we can see that the dawn of philosophy is a very definite staging post in the development of the human being. The years 1400-1500 AD are another. This is the beginning of the modern age and the understanding of nature through intellectual natural science, which has led to modern technological developments. At the same time it marks a point in history where people have a greater feeling of themselves as individualities.

We can, therefore, trace historically the development of humanity from a period when the soul had an instinctive connection with the spiritual, through a time when there were intermediaries in the form of priests, to the present almost wholly materialistic civilization. It is too easy to think of earlier peoples as inferior to our "clever" selves. The fact is that they were different and had different experiences. For instance, it is believed that, physically, the ancient Egyptians were much stronger than people of today. From their engravings it would also appear that they had no sense of perspective. The Greeks experienced colors and tones differently. In music, for instance, they had a pentatonic scale.

In considering the immense possibilities in the teaching of history, it is little short of criminal to set before children a short and limited extract, such as is so often done in the schools. This must have the effect of circumscribing and confining the mind which in itself is infinite. As geography leads to an understanding of oneself in space, so history leads to an understanding in time. Thus we consider it a good thing to teach history but we must still consider how it fits in with the general aims of education.

Education as a whole seeks to teach skills, to awaken social responsibility and to further individual development. History has a place in the general scheme, but perhaps it has a particular purpose in that it gives the human being a picture of him- or herself as the end of a long process and shows how modern life has within it the achievements of past civilizations. There is the smaller aspect of his or her everyday job and environment, but there is the larger one of his or her place in the world order. The school curriculum cannot encompass the story of all past civilizations, their economics, politics, etc., but proper history teaching can show the individual his or her place. History can teach objective evaluation; it can show a pattern in existence. In showing how the past is here in the present, it may give ideas for the future. In history it can be shown how impulses manifest themselves and that the human being is not necessarily pushed about by economic or political forces. It would seem today as if humanity had become a pawn of these forces, yet we must try to realize that we ourselves are history, and make history. Marx declared that we are the products of our environment but he, as an individual, belied his own statement.

History is a vast subject and to teach only bits and pieces of it is not very satisfactory. It is obvious, therefore, that the teaching must be in broad outline and that there must be economy. The widest picture must be given in the shortest time. (We are not speaking in terms of specialist studies.) It is quite possible to take a whole period and develop a feeling for the important events of this period within the space of a few weeks. Such a one in this sense could be the Greek civilization or the Roman world. In dealing with the Greeks, it is not only a matter of describing outer events (indeed, this is less important), but of giving a picture of the general trend. That is to say, one gives the basic characteristics of Greek history, the character of the Greek, some information about the cities' regulations, arts, the general contribution of the Greeks to human development, and one shows what here in the present is derived from them, e.g., culture, politics, the Greek words in our language. Thus, history is not taught as something abstract and divorced from humanity and from the present. What we have in the present is at least a partial legacy of the past.

Pictorial representations of events, and particularly of people, will evoke the greatest response, especially in the pre-puberty years. It is a matter of characterizing, not defining. Vivid descriptions of events and personalities are the required food. But it is not only a question of giving the picture of a particular period, but of finding and describing the inner impulses of which the events appear as symptoms. For instance, the Greek impulse was towards individuality and democracy. Symptoms are the Persian wars and the facial expressions in the Greek statues. At the time of the Reformation there is a still stronger urge towards independent thinking, coupled with growing interest in the physical world. As with all subjects, the teaching of history must be structured to harmonize with the child's stages of development. Let us briefly recapitulate these.

Up to the age of nine the child is still in something of a dream. At nine, some interest awakens for the outer world and a greater understanding for it at twelve. At fourteen come the powers of independent perception and judgement. During the years from six to fourteen, the pictorial descriptive approach touches the child most deeply. From fourteen onwards there can be reasoning and rationalization. To accord with the child's development, the history syllabus will be as follows:

From six to nine there is no history proper. Single stories can be told with historical background but there should be no attempt at sequence. At the age of nine or ten, the history is still interwoven with the period we call "study of home surroundings." This is a geographical-historical study of the immediate environment. It should provide an experience of how the particular locality has grown in time—the changes that have taken place and the reasons, insofar as they can be understood. This period will provide the opportunity of presenting many historical as well as geographical concepts.

In the next year the study branches out into definite subjects, of which history is one. It is at this stage (age eleven) that the contents of this booklet become relevant. The child now has an awareness of time, but no logical faculty. Pictures in the mind are still the most potent form of educational material and, since history has its beginnings in mythology, Ancient Indian, Persian and Egyptian mythologies and stories, plus those of Greece and Rome (where there is also more historical evidence), will take us through age eleven to the turning point of twelve. The age of twelve brings a marked development of the bony system and a feeling of independence. The material civilization of the Romans and their insistence on law fit this age of the child. It is worth repeating that, in general, up to the age of twelve, complete pictures or biographies or descriptions of characteristic events will be most effective. As with other subjects, what children love in these years, they will understand later. Let there be, therefore, a stimulation of sympathy (or antipathy, for in this sense, one can also love what is antipathetic) since these will work at a deeper level. In particular, biographies will be very helpful. Historical ideas are skeletons, but living deeds, events and human beings are the flesh and blood of history.

At the ages of thirteen and fourteen comes the beginning of conceptual thinking. The great change marked by the Reformation and the beginnings of modern natural science parallel in history this human development. After fourteen, one can begin to deal with reasons, causes, effects and historical motives of this most important period and proceed up to modern times. In the upper school, all history should be reviewed in the light of understanding. The process should be: exposition in the earlier years, explanations in the later. Finally, a survey of present cultures should be given as, for example, the contrasts between America and China. (This could also be done in the geography lessons if more convenient.)

In the time available in Classes five and six, it is not possible to give all the details which one might wish, neither is it necessary; but the quality of these can be conveyed. In the case of India and Persia, there is also the further difficulty of fixing dates due to lack of external evidence, but in the stories there are references to matters which obviously lie far back in time.

Ancient India

We will try first of all to give a few general indications as to the nature of Ancient India culled from the literature available, and suggest a few stories which are especially useful. Something about the land itself can be included.

India is ten times the size of the British Isles and is shaped like a triangle. From north to south it stretches about 1500 miles and nearly the same from east to west. It has the sea on two sides, and across its northern boundary lies the huge mass of the Himalayas. Just south of these mountains are the three great rivers and their plains—the Ganges, Indus and the Brahmaputra. India teems with life. Not only is there an enormous population, but there is abundant animal and plant life. There are jungles in which are found monkeys, tigers, elephants, snakes and crocodiles. In the plains, crops such as maize, wheat, rice, tea and cocoa can be grown. In some parts it can be unbelievably hot and unbelievably dry. Although most of the people live in what we should think are very backward rural conditions, there are roads, railways, industries and teeming cities: but it was not always like this. These are modern developments just as they are in other parts of the world.

Thousands of years ago, India was peopled by mixtures of dark-skinned races, but then a great invasion and colonization took place from the north. The people that came in as conquerors were called the Aryans. They came from the mountains to the north of India and there is an old legend which tells how they came there. This is a story similar to that of Noah and, according to some authorities, it relates to the sinking of Atlantis about the year 10,000 BC, after which a new type of people developed.

Once upon a time a holy Rishi (teacher) named Manu was walking by a brook when a fish rose up from the stream and asked for protection. He took it home. The fish grew bigger and bigger and finally asked to be put into the sea. This was done and then it said, "Build an ark, take samples of all seeds, take the seven holy Rishis. There will be a flood. I will appear as a horned animal. When you see me, follow me."

All this happened and the horned fish towed the ark to dry land and then revealed itself as the God, Brahma. He then gave instructions to Manu about how all things were to be recreated.

Manu's people were of fairer skin and they came into a country of many races. Some mixing of the bloodlines took place but, in order to preserve purity, the priests (Brahmins) divided the people into four classes (castes), which really represented social functions. These were:

- The Brahmins   Priests, directors of science and religion
- The Kshattriyas   Kings, warriors, administrators
- The Vaisyas   Farmers, merchants, craftsmen
- The Sudras   Aboriginals, servants (later known as
                      Pariahs)

These divisions were rigid but have no justification in the present age of humanity.

Many stories of India have been handed down and it is difficult to say to which period they belong. But from these stories and the references in them, we can deduce quite a different state of mind and understanding from ours. There is a continual interweaving of gods and human beings. The gods appear in human form. People are able to perceive and hold converse with the gods. There is an oft-repeated theme of hardships undergone and sacrifices made in order to attain the higher worlds. Renunciation, bowing to the will of the gods, is another theme. There are references to reincarnation and to the sins of a former life bringing misfortunes in this. Human beings are endowed with celestial weapons and have power over the elements. Demons abound. Nature and the world are peopled by gods and spirits. Emotions are caused by supersensible beings. There is little feeling of self-responsibility. The ego is not awake. From the stories, the Indian cosmogony and beliefs can be divined. At the beginning of the story of Rama, as told by the French writer Schuré, we find:

Heaven is my father. He it was who begat me. My family consists of all this heavenly company. The great earth is my mother. The highest part of its surface is her womb; there the father fecundates her who is at once his bride and his daughter.

Thus is expressed the double origin of humanity. The divine is higher than the terrestrial. The origin of the soul is celestial. The body is the product of earth, fertilized by the cosmos. Schuré also explains how the people felt that their goods, even sons and daughters, were bestowed on them by the godhead. A belief in different epochs is also expressed, in the so-called Yugas. In the first of these there were no religions, no gods, no religious ceremonies, no demons, no poor, no rich, no need to labor. All was obtained by power of will. There was no disease and there were no worldly desires. This would appear to refer to a paradisaical state since there was no disease, hence a time before the human spirit entered matter, the physical body.

References to reincarnation are numerous. One person wants to reincarnate for a certain purpose. Another recognizes that the misfortunes of this life are due to some sin in a previous one. These things are talked about as everyday fact. The *Bhagavad Gita* also expresses the idea of the Kingdom of Heaven.

> Nay, but as when one layeth
> His worn out robes away
> And taking new ones sayeth,
> "These will I wear today."
> So putteth by the spirit
> Lightly its garb of flesh,
> And passeth to inherit
> A residence afresh.
>   (Translation by Edwin Arnold)

There is also a timeless aspect. Time appears to mean little. A banishment of fourteen years is nothing and, in the same stream of experience, is the ever-recurring theme of renunciation or acceptance of fate. A certain person turns aside and refrains from helping another because he recognizes that the destiny of the latter is being fulfilled. To the ancient Indian, life on earth was a banishment from the celestial fields for which he longed.

> Every moment the voice of love comes from left and right,
> But here on earth is darkness—grant us eternal light.
> We have lived in heaven, the angels were our friends.
> Thither let us go, for there our suffering ends.

We also find the idea that the gods can incarnate on the human plane. Thus at various stages of need, Vishnu incarnates. The hero, Rama, is an incarnation of Vishnu. So is Krishna. Another theme is that of the holy men who live as Anchorites in a state of asceticism and thus achieve wisdom.

There are many beautiful stories in Indian mythology which can be told in full or from which episodes can be extracted by way of illustration. In the story of Nala and Damayanti we read that Nala is on his way to woo Damayanti when four gods appear to him. These are: Indra, lord of heaven; Agni, god of fire; Varuna, god of waters; Yama, god of death. They ask him to announce to Damayanti that they themselves are coming for the same purpose. The gods take on the same form as Nala, but as the gods do not blink or cast a shadow, Damayanti can recognize Nala and she chooses him. The gods are pleased at her steadfastness and bestow on Nala their gifts, i.e., he gains mastery of the elements.

In another story, Arjuna, one of the Pandava brothers, was taken to the celestial mansions of the great god Indra, and given a javelin that could be hurled by the mind. Yama gave him his mace, against which none can stand. He was also given a weapon which sent the foe to sleep.

Rama was the leader of the Aryans who conquered India. He was an initiate with magical powers. He made a spring come forth in the desert. He could produce a sort of Manna. He could heal and create illusions in other people. He perceived Deva Nahushu, the divine intelligence, who explained to him the constellations and the destiny of human beings from the Zodiac. Thus, we see how gods and human beings walk side by side, and how human beings possess magical gifts, and it is obvious that the human powers, faculties and understanding were very different from ours.

The gods are active in all things, both in nature and in the human being. There are many gods and their functions sometimes appear to overlap, but we must remember that we are dealing with a vast period of time and a huge complex of peoples, so that names and functions may come and go or interchange. What is certain, however, is the fact that the people had a realization of a divine presence, whatever terms were used.

Brahma was the creator, the writer of destiny, what we might look upon as a God-Father, the father principle. Vishnu was of the substance of Brahma and seems to have had a special interest in humankind. Indra was known as the king of the gods. He was the thunderer, god of fertility, friend of mankind, artisan of the universe, dragon-slayer, god of war. Indra fashioned the universe. He built the world walls and left doors for the gods to enter. He was helped by the nature spirits such as Agni, the god of fire, who provided the vital spark in the human being. Vata, Rudra, were wind gods. Varuna ruled over the waters. There was a sun god, Surya. Saraswathi, or Vani, was the wife of Brahma and the goddess of speech and learning. Lakshmi, wife of Vishnu, was the goddess of wealth. Yama was the god of death. Shiva was the destroyer and Kali, his wife, the goddess of desire. With Kali's favor, one could control demons and evil spirits that could possess humanity. There were also endless evil spirits known as the Rakshasas or Asuras. These were the workers of evil, darkness, drought. In the story of Nala, an evil spirit is able to enter him because he overlooked some ritual. A god known as Rahu swallows the sun and moon—perhaps what we should call an eclipse. The human being can combat these evil beings with charms and exhortations. The Rakshasas desire to mislead the human race. They disturb people, for instance, at their prayers, and this is the theme at the beginning of the *Ramayana*.

There are not only struggles between humans and demons, but also between gods and demons. There is, for instance, the story of Indra fighting the demon of drought, Vritri. There is a wonderful touch in this story illustrative of the Indian's disregard of the physical. Indra had a magic weapon which was made from the bones of a sinless man who gave up his body for the purpose.

The manly deeds of Indra shall be sung.
The first was when the thunderstone he flung
And smote the dragon.
He released the fountains;
He oped the channels of the breasted mountains.
With magic weapon he rode out to meet the foe
He killed the demon Vritri with one blow,
And, like to bellowing cattle rushing free
The gladsome waters then descended to the sea.
Around the monster torrents surged,
Nor paused, nor stayed, but ever onward urged.
They covered Vritri by a joyful wave
And bore him to a darksome ocean grave.

The above may give some idea of background and some material for understanding the Ancient Indian civilization.

According to taste and opportunity, including the time factor, the teacher can then tell stories. There is an opportunity in the Upper School to enter into the more philosophical understanding of these things. For the present, one gives information, descriptions and stories of which the following are abridged examples.

RAMA AND SITA

Once upon a time there was an evil spirit called Ravana, King of the Rakshasas. He was a torment to the people and disturbed them at their prayers. At last, Brahma was asked to intervene and Brahma said that only an earthly man could overcome him. Then Vishnu, one of the gods, took it upon himself to be born as a man in order to destroy Ravana.

There was a certain king upon the earth who had three wives but no sons. Special prayers were offered for an heir and all three wives had sons, one of whom was the incarnated Vishnu. His name on earth was Rama.

Rama grew up to be a great favorite with everyone, and all the people wanted him to rule after his father's death, with one exception. The one against him was the mother of one of the other princes who wanted her son to be king. She came to the king and reminded him how he had promised her anything she wished when she had nursed him in sickness. Now, she said, she would like that promise fulfilled and this was that her son should be named as heir to the throne. This prince himself, however, did not agree and thought that Rama was the one who should eventually reign. Nevertheless, it was agreed that Rama should be sent away for fourteen years.

Rama left, and in his wanderings he came to a strange city where there was a mighty bow. It was said that whoever could bend the bow and hit a certain target should marry the Princess Sita. Many had tried and failed but Rama was successful, and Sita became his bride. They went to live in a hut in the forest but, one day when Rama was out, Ravana came and stole Sita away. Then there was great rejoicing in heaven, for now the gods knew that Rama would slay the evil one.

Rama searched for a long time in vain. He asked Hanuman, the king of the monkeys, for aid. Hanuman sent his messengers out in all directions and finally news was brought that Sita had been carried away to an island in the south.

Rama, Hanuman, and all his people set out to rescue her. They came to the sea and Rama called up the king of the ocean for permission to cross. This was granted, and the monkeys built a bridge by linking themselves together. Then began a fearful battle with the Rakshasas. The sun was darkened and the earth shook. By day, the monkeys seemed victorious by night, the Rakshasas. Gradually, however, Rama and his friends overcame the evil spirits and Rama himself slew Ravana. Then Rama and Sita returned to their country and ruled it until it was time for them to leave the earth.

KRISHNA

After a time, Vishnu came again to the earth as the great teacher and helper, Krishna. At that time there was a very wicked king called Kansa. It was foretold to him that a boy who would soon be born to certain parents would destroy him. This boy was Krishna. Kansa, therefore, shut the parents up in a dungeon, intending to kill the child when it was born. However, as soon as the child made its appearance, the parents heard a voice telling them to escape. They were to take the child to a farmer to be brought up. Miraculously, the doors of the prison opened. Outside, a jackal led them towards a river, the level of which dropped as soon as the boy touched the waters with his foot, so that they were able to cross.

Once on the farm, a wicked witch disguised as a kind lady offered to suckle the child but, when she touched him, immediately her beauty left her and her true form was seen.

Another time a demon tried to roll a cart on the boy but he pushed it back and killed the demon.

While still a child, he overcame a demon in a whirlwind. He pulled over two great trees and released two good spirits which had been bound there by enchantment. He slew a demon sheep which attacked him and he purified the waters of a poisonous lake by conquering the hundred-headed snake which lived there.

When a forest fire broke out, he drew it to himself in three great mouthfuls and put it out. He moved a mountain to save people when a flood threatened.

When he was twelve, he was invited to wrestle at the king's court. The king already suspected that this was the one who would fulfill the prophecy, and he gave secret orders that the boy should be killed as if by accident. However, Krishna was victorious and his opponents fled. Then Krishna leapt to the place where the king was seated and put his hand on the king's head. The crown rolled off and Kansa fell lifeless.

THE PANDAVAS

At one time in a certain kingdom there was a great struggle over the heir to the throne. Princes, called the Pandavas, were the rightful successors, but the Kuravas had taken the kingdom from them. At last, it came to a great battle between them.

Yudishthira and Arjuna were two of the leaders of the Pandavas who were helped by Krishna. Arjuna was one who knew who Krishna really was and, just before the battle began, Krishna showed himself to Arjuna in his heavenly form. In one moment, Arjuna understood the hidden causes of things and the secrets of birth and death, but it took him all the rest of his lifetime to write them down.

After the battle was over, a great light seemed to come down from the heavens. Indra came to comfort the women whose relatives had been killed. Krishna told them to remember that the spirit of a human being lives forever. It was then seen that the dead from both sides arose as friends, were met by Indra and taken into his heaven.

THE STORY OF THE BUDDHA

Once a king named Sudhodana had a son. He was called Siddhartha and his family name was Gautama. He had lived many lives on earth and had suffered and endured and had grown wiser than other men. The priests said that he would become a wise man but his father wanted him to become an emperor. The priests said that if he saw suffering he would remember his past and then want to help the sufferer. Only if he did not see sickness, disease or death, would he become a ruler. Accordingly, the king tried to keep him from seeing these things, but one day Gautama went out and saw sick, diseased, and dead people. Then he knew that he would have to seek enlightenment. He left his palace, wife and child, and went to talk with hermits and holy men. He sat for seven days and seven nights under the bo-tree, thinking and praying. Demons tried to disturb him, but his thoughts had made a circle round him which protected him.

He gained the knowledge he sought and then became a great teacher. In his teaching he said that only lasting happiness can be obtained by leaving behind life on earth and entering the peace called Nirvana. Gautama came to be known as "The Buddha," that is, "The Enlightened One."

SAVITRI AND SATYAVAN

The princess Savitri decides on a journey to find her future husband. She meets Satyavan and knows immediately "that her destiny was come upon her. Here stood the soul to whom through endless births she had been united."

She comes back to her father with the news and he is pleased, but the sage at the court is disturbed and advises against the union, since Satyavan is destined to die a year hence. Nevertheless, Savitri insists, and the marriage takes place. She goes to live with Satyavan in the forest, accompanied by his blind father and aged mother, who are a king and a queen deprived of their kingdom.

A year to the day, Savitri and Satyavan are in the forest, when Satyavan lies down complaining of a headache. Yama, the god of death, comes and leads him away. Savitri follows. Yama turns and admonishes her; nevertheless, he offers her a gift since she is so steadfast in her love. She asks for the restoration of sight for her blind father-in-law, which is granted. Yama departs and Savitri follows. Again he chides her but again offers a gift. She asks that the old king and queen be restored to their kingdom. It is granted.

Yama continues on his way and still Savitri follows. Again he remonstrates and again promises her a gift, but suggests that this time she should choose something for herself.

"Many sons," she says.

"Granted," answers Yama.

"But a widow does not remarry," she replies.

Yama is tricked, but pleased. He says, "Peerless among women is that brave heart that follows the husband even into the grave and recovers his life from Yama himself. Thus do the gods love to win defeat at the hands of the mortals."

Ancient Persia

The next period shows that the scene has shifted westwards and that another race of people are in the lead who take a further step towards the material world. Ancient Persia, or Iran, is now the center of events.

Geographically, a birds-eye view of the country would show a high plateau broken by valleys and rocky gorges with huge mountains to the north and east. There are forests on the mountainsides, green oases in the valleys, and arid deserts. It is a picture of savage grandeur. There are no great rivers so water must be obtained from underground sources. The land is full of contrasts. It is stormy in spring; from May to September it is dry, and during this period the atmosphere is pure. Summer is warm and peaceful, winter fierce and terrible.

Fruit trees and crops grow in the valleys and where irrigation is possible. On the mountainsides there is deep snow, and wildlife consists of bears and vultures. The land suggests the idea of struggle and resistance. It only yields fruit through hard work. It is a land where life is an eternal fight with nature.

ZARATHUSTRA

The story of Persian civilization centers around the personality of Zarathustra, or Zoroaster, as he was known to the Greeks. Different authorities give different dates for his existence, and the name may have been used repeatedly and legends woven around him as in the case of King Arthur. It is nevertheless possible to characterize the epoch through stories of the life and the work of Zarathustra, although one great leader precedes him.

A legend says that Ahura Mazdao, the great god who lived in the light of the sun, gave Yima, one of the first leaders of the Persian people, a golden sword with which he was to draw a furrow. (Yima appears in some stories under the name of Djemjid). This points to a change of direction as compared with ancient India. Human beings are being directed towards the things of the earth. They become cultivators and cattle raisers. However, Yima, who was possessed of great spiritual powers, turned towards evil, and another leader appeared—Zarathustra, priest, soldier-king, shepherd and farmer. Whereas Buddha is typical of India's turning from the earthly world to seclusion in order to attain a higher world by means of meditation, it is obvious from the legends of Zarathustra that the soul attitude here is towards the earth, to find contacts with the gods through deeds, living in perpetual battle with the evil forces.

When it was known that Zarathustra was to be born, all nature rejoiced—all the plants and animals. At his actual birth it became so light around the house that the whole village was illuminated. The evil demons wanted to attack the house but they were stopped by the good powers and fled into the underworld. The child laughed and was able to speak at birth; but the evil powers tried to destroy him. A great sorcerer drew his dagger and tried to stab him, but his arm was paralyzed. The child was kidnapped and put into the midst of a pile of dry wood which was set on fire, but he slept in the middle of the fire unharmed. He was put on a cattle track and oxen were driven along it, but the first ox stood guard over him. The same thing happened with horses. His opponents put him in a wolves' lair and destroyed the cubs, but when the wolves attacked him, their jaws locked. When he was fifteen, he declared his loathing of sorcery and his intention to combat it, and he demanded the sacred cord of priesthood. At twenty-one he left home.

In ancient times Persia was inhabited by two different peoples, the Aryans and the Turanians. The Turanians, yellow-skinned, with small cunning eyes, worshipped the god Ahriman, the prince of darkness. The Aryans saw their god in the light of the sun and named him Ahura Mazdao, the Great Light. The Turanians had conquered the country and the Aryans lived as scattered tribes.

One day, a prince of the Aryans called Arjasp came into a beautiful valley at the end of which flowed a crystal clear spring of water. By the side of the spring stood the figure of a woman. Arjasp asked of the woman, "To whom does this spring belong?"

"It belongs to Vahumano, the sage, the guardian of the fire and the servant of the highest," she replied.

"And thy name?" asked Arjasp.

"I am called Ardouizur, which means 'the source of light,' and I am named after this spring," said the woman, "but be careful should you drink of this water; for whosoever drinks will have an unquenchable thirst which only a god can satisfy."

The woman disappeared among the trees. Arjasp drank of the waters and went on his way.

Years passed, and the Turanian leader ordered all people to come to acknowledge his sovereignty in the temple of Ahriman. At the ceremony, Arjasp was horrified to see Ardouizur given to one of the chieftains. It was impossible for him to rescue her, but as she was carried away he recalled her words at the spring, and the burning thirst came over him to save her and the rest of the Aryan race from their evil oppressors.

Arjasp sought the advice of Vahumano. He promised to give up everything and do anything necessary to fulfill his task. Vahumano told him that he must disappear from his people, climb to a mountaintop, and there let his thoughts dwell on the great Sun Spirit, who would speak to him in time. Vahumano gave him another name, Zarathustra, which means "splendor of the sun."

Zarathustra spent ten years on the mountain. He was guarded by an eagle, a bull and a lion. He was tempted by evil spirits who also tried to terrify him. The thought of Ardouizur haunted him. Then, one night, the Spirit of Light, Ahura Mazdao himself, appeared to him, and from that time onward he was always able to speak with him. With Ahura Mazdao as guide, Zarathustra taught and led his people, until finally after forty years' struggle, the Turanians were vanquished.

When it was time for Zarathustra to leave the earth, he climbed the mountain and saw a beautiful golden bridge in front of him. On it stood the radiant figure of Ardouizur to welcome him. As he turned to look back at the earth, he had a vision of things to happen in the future. He saw the Aryan peoples marching on victoriously towards the west, and at their head was the spirit figure of Ardouizur.

Zarathustra taught his people to tend the earth, otherwise the spirits of darkness would take possession of it. Agriculture was a sacred duty. Evil forces could enter into any patch of uncultivated ground. This was the period of the domestication of animals. The Persians learned how to raise sheep and use their wool, to tame horses as their servants, to make friends with the dog. They cultivated the wild grasses which became the grains, and produced edible fruit from wild varieties.

Another sacred duty of the Persians was to speak the truth. Lying meant helping Ahriman in his struggle to overthrow Ahura Mazdao. In the holy book of the Persians, the *Zend Avesta*, there is an explanation of what happens when a good person dies and when an evil person dies. The good person is met by a beautiful maiden who says, "I am thy conscience. I have become fair through thy good thought, speech and actions." The evil person is met by a hideous old woman who says, "I am made like this by thy evil thoughts, speech and actions. Thou hast made me hideous and vile."

The *Zend Avesta* also records a conversation between Zarathustra and Ahura Mazdao which illustrates very well the importance of agriculture.

Zarathustra: O Maker of the World, what is the first thing which gives most pleasure to the earth?

Ahura Mazdao: When a pure man walks over the earth.

Zarathustra: O Maker of the World, what is the second thing which gives most pleasure to the earth?

Ahura Mazdao: When a pure man builds a house.

Zarathustra: O Maker of the World, what is the third thing which gives most pleasure to the earth?

Ahura Mazdao: When there is a fire and women and children.

Zarathustra: O Maker of the World, what is the fourth thing
                 which gives most pleasure to the earth?

Ahura Mazdao: When there are fine cattle and good flocks.

Zarathustra: O Maker of the World, what is the fifth thing
                 which gives most pleasure to the earth?

Ahura Mazdao: When there is growing good corn and fine fruits.

Thus again, without intellectual explanation, it can be conveyed
that something new developed in the Persian epoch, and also
that something was lost. We see the new impulse as being directed towards the physical earth, and we also see the emergence of
a leader who could walk and talk with the god only after great
preparation, i.e., the spiritual world was not immediately present
but had to be attained through initiation. Humanity was still led
by one who had to seek his source of inspiration from the deity.

Egypt and Babylonia

We now have to deal with the next great civilization, the great
complex of the river valley cultures of the Nile, Tigris and
Euphrates. The countries concerned are Egypt, Assyria,
Babylonia and Chaldea. It is not possible to deal with them all in
detail; neither is it necessary or desirable. There was a uniformi-
ty in the culture and, for our purposes here, we shall deal with
Egypt and Babylonia. Geographically speaking, Chaldea was the
southern part of Babylonia. Mention might be made of the
Chaldeans, a name eventually given to the learned men versed in
Babylonian astronomy and astrology.

We shall see now how a further step is taken from the spiritual world into matter. We are now able to take more tangible historical evidence into account and, both from this and the legends,

we can see how the nature of consciousness is changing—from spirit to matter.

There are many interesting things that can be described here since there are records. One can describe the lands themselves and the way of living but, bearing in mind our theme and limitations of time, it is advisable not to be too ambitious.

Egypt has a long and complicated history. In considering the civilization which developed here, we are not attempting to depict historical events and sequences, but rather we are trying to give an idea of the essence of Egyptian culture. During the course of the years there were many political developments and changes, and an apparently great confusion of gods and beliefs. However, we are dealing with a great span of time and it must be remembered that cultures have a beginning, a rise, a peak, and then a fall. The beginning of a period of culture may appear chaotic. Indeed, it usually is, for there are conquests and reconquests, a going and a coming of peoples and a mixing of the blood. From the intermingling of races, something new develops—new faculties of the mind, a new consciousness.

The peak of Egyptian culture was probably between 2700 and 1465 BC, and during this period everything was centered in religion. The Pharaoh was state and god, and this is one of the important aspects. There is a religious revolution with Akhenaton in 1415 BC, and then a steady decline.

In presenting Egypt to children of ages 11 and 12, there are many interesting external facts to relate as well as stories. Some indication as to the significance of these stories is given here but this, of course, is not for the children at this stage.

A very good start can be made by speaking of matters about which they already know something, i.e., Biblical references. They will know about Moses in the bulrushes, Joseph sold into slavery, and the flight of Joseph, Mary and the baby Jesus. They may have heard familiar expressions such as "corn in the land of Egypt," and "making bricks without straw."

The next thing meriting some description is the land itself. Civilizations develop in, and are connected with, certain locations. The third cultural epoch took place in the river valleys of the Nile, Tigris and Euphrates, a very different setting from that of Persia.

It has been said that Egypt is a gift of the Nile, and as far as landscape is concerned, the river is certainly the main feature. In the upper reaches, there are rocks such as granite, limestone, basalt and sandstone. Lower down, the land is flat, presents an enormous horizon, and the ever-present sun burns in the copper sky. There is no rainfall.

The ancient Egyptians relied on the river for irrigating the land which then became extremely fertile, but beyond the immediate banks of the river there was desert. The river flooded the land for about a hundred days each year and left behind a rich layer of silt. The people, knowing nothing of the melting of the snows a few thousand miles away at the source of the Nile, attributed the flood to the god Hapi:

> Hail to thee, Hapi, who comest
> Giving life unto Egypt.
> Thou didst hide thy coming in darkness.
> The day of thy coming is secret.
> Bring life to all that do thirst
> Refuse to give drink to the desert—
> Overflow, water of heaven.
> Sibu, the Earth-God, awaits thee.

The overflowing of the river determined the divisions of the year. This fell into three parts—flood, growing, harvesting—and each period lasted for three to four months. Flood time was from June to September. The growing season followed and harvesting took place from March onwards.

Seeds were sown as soon as the waters receded. They were lightly plowed in by oxen; pigs and sheep were driven over the ground to trample them in. The soil was then raked over. The Egyptians grew a good many vegetable crops with which we are also familiar: onions, leeks, beans, garlic, lentils, radishes, spinach, turnips, carrots, lettuce, cucumbers and gourds. Fruits were: figs, dates, apples, pomegranates, melons, grapes. Grain crops were wheat, barley and millet.

The people ate meat such as beef, lamb, goat and poultry. They ate fish and eggs, made butter, cheese, bread and cake. They drank milk, wine and beer.

Clothes in the hot climate were very sparse and simple, but people adorned themselves with fancy jewelry such as necklaces and bead collars. They used cosmetics.

With regard to housing, wood and stone were scarce in some parts of the land, and the ordinary folk lived in houses built of bricks made of mud and straw. Lintels and beams were also made of mud strengthened with strips of linen. Panels were made by the same process. Floors were covered with gypsum. The richer citizens had chairs, tables and beds, but the peasants had no furniture.

The Egyptians had an astounding skill in crafts and a great variety of craftsmen. They had stonemasons and metalworkers in copper whose only means of melting the metal was by lung power. Goldsmiths also worked in the same way. The potter's wheel was known, and the kiln. There were carvers of ivory and wood, glass-blowers, painters, mat and basket makers whose raw material was palm leaves. Flax was grown and hence thread, ropes and linen were manufactured. Boats were made of timber floated from the Lebanon. Paper was made from the papyrus reed. Among the tools and implements in use were saws, chisels, ladles, forceps, razors and surgical instruments. Soldiers were armed with spears, clubs, daggers and battle-axes.

Transport was mainly by water, and all sorts of boats were in use, both sailing and rowing. Palanquins were used for carrying the richer people. In later times chariots were used both for hunting and for war purposes.

The Egyptians built enormous temples of stone. They erected pyramids and carved out tombs from the solid rock for their kings. Certain of them understood the art of healing, dentistry, mathematics and geometry, astrology and astronomy. Among them were musicians and they had stringed musical instruments, flutes, drums, bells and long trumpets of brass or copper.

Business was conducted both by means of barter and money, and there was a banking system. The counting system was different from ours. The Egyptians counted in tens and units, and had no numbers two to nine. Thus:

$13 = 10+1+1+1$

$124 = 100+10+10+1+1+1+1$

$2354 = 1000+1000+100+100+100+10+10+10+10+10+1+1+ 1+1$

The Egyptian calendar began with the rising of the star Sirius at the height of the Nile flood. There were twelve months in the year, of thirty days each, and five extra days were added for festivals in connection with agriculture.

They had a form of writing known as hieroglyphics, which means "sacred writing." It was known only to the priests. It did not consist of letters put together to make words, like our western languages, but was made up of pictures. The scribe, i.e., one skilled in these matters, was very important, and a scribe had an open door to all other professions.

⊙   means the sun, or light, or time

≈≈   means waves, water, river, sea, or wash

Society was ordered by the priests under the priest-king, the Pharaoh. Peasants had to give time to their master's ground and to public works. During the time of the flood they had to work on the pyramids. This was acceptable to the people because at that time there was very little feeling of self-consciousness, that is to say, the individual was not particularly conscious of his own individuality and did not act out of his own feeling of ego.

The Pharaoh was half-god, priest-king, and all life was arranged by him and his priests. It is interesting to note how the temples were the centers of everything and on what enormous scale they functioned. For instance, two temples at Thebes had 90,000 workmen, 500,000 head of cattle, 400 orchards, 80 ships and 50 workshops. They drew income from 65 of the most prosperous towns in Egypt and in the Egyptian Empire in Palestine.

There was no separation into religious, political and economic life. The priests took care of all. They ordered the time for sowing and harvesting. They arranged work and were the rulers. People, either noblemen or peasants, were content with their lot because they trusted the wisdom of their leaders. Sculptors, painters, craftsmen, worked as a team, with little feeling for themselves as individuals. All people agreed in the ordering of society, which was divinely inspired. They felt horror at isolation.

There is a rather plaintive story from Egypt of a brickmaker who dies of boredom because he has to work alone. It is entitled "The Dialogue of a Man with his Soul." All have deserted him; he has nobody to speak to. Life is not worth living. He dreads dying because of the darkness and solitude of the tomb which awaits him. The soul is deserting him.

The priest-initiates obviously possessed special powers—what we might call today supersensible powers. The so-called "temple sleep" was a sort of hypnotic process by which the priest-physicians dimmed the consciousness of the patient and controlled the pictures that arose in the soul. Harmony stimulated the life forces in the body and thus a healing process was achieved. They also had some special power in the *word*. Evil spirits could be cast out by those who knew their names, i.e., recognized them.

It has always been a matter of conjecture as to how the pyramids were built. According to Dr. Steiner, the priests were able to exert an hypnotic power on the workmen through the spoken word which produced extra strength.

In order to obtain special powers or spiritual vision, it was necessary to undergo "initiation." This means that suitable people were chosen who had to undergo a very rigorous training and were then put into a sort of trance in which they became aware of a supersensible world, i.e., they came into direct contact with the divine powers. They were then able to draw their inspiration from this source. It is generally assumed that the pyramids were the tombs of the pharaohs. No body has ever been found in a pyramid, and the assumption may be wrong. An early text says of the pyramid: "A staircase to heaven is laid for Pharaoh that he may ascend to heaven thereby." This may well be taken to mean that the pyramid was a place of initiation for the Pharaoh.

Through their inspirations, which brought them into direct contact with the spiritual world, the priests were able to guide and order a harmonious society. They acted in accordance with the constellations, even to the extent of deciding on the ancestry for the new Pharaohs. The close blood relationship was necessary to conserve certain powers. From their spiritual insight, the priests could determine suitable state leaders or future priests.

The king, Pharaoh, was a reflection of the sun. The crown was a manifestation of supersensible rays—the halo—which radiated from the head of the initiate. The people saw god in the king.

Let us now try to penetrate further into the state of mind of people at this time. We have spoken of history as being the evolution of consciousness. In ancient times, people were aware of a spiritual world, but the faculty of penetrating into this world receded, and humans became more and more aware of the physical world until, finally, the spiritual vision was lost. A new power took its place, namely, thinking. In the third cultural epoch, there was an awareness of the downward path into matter, and the story of the founding of Egyptian culture gives us a clue as to the new human powers to be developed.

The first king was called Menes. The word is cognate with the Sanskrit *manas*, which refers to "the thinking man." The same root is in Manu, also in Minos, where the labyrinth, characterizing the human brain, was built. We shall refer to this later in dealing with the Greek epoch. Menes, therefore, represents the man, used in the general sense of the human being, whose conception of the world changes from spiritual vision to that of independent thought.

With the loss of spiritual perception comes a realization of mortality, and hence the Egyptians' preoccupation with the idea of death and of life beyond death.

They spoke of a "golden age"—a time when the gods lived on earth—but what this really means is that the human race was aware of the spiritual world and its inhabitants. The evidence of the dimming of the supersensible faculties is found in the story of Ra and his departure from this world. Ra was the great god, the sun-god, the ruler, but Ra grew old. Before he left the earth, he married a mortal woman and their descendants were the Pharaohs. Ra had an eye separable from himself, and the Pharaohs wore this symbol on their foreheads as a sign of majesty and descent from Ra. In the hieroglyphic script:

= eye, = see, = know, = awake

The Pharaohs and the priests were able to attain spiritual vision through initiation, i.e., their souls were projected into the supersensible world. For the mass of the people, the immediate vision was fading but a memory and a feeling for the existence of a spiritual world remained.

Thus the Egyptians had an instinctive belief in gods and spirits and in a life after death where there would be a judgement. They believed in the spiritual being of man as well as the physical. They believed that the human being was a divine creation. Whereas the Bible tells us of God breathing the breath of life into Adam, Egyptian sources tell us that the human being was endowed with the gift of a *Ka* by the sun-god, Ra. He lives while his Ka is with him. The Ka could leave the body during sleep and meet the dead. It existed in the body during life and continued its existence into after-life.

We said that the entry by the mind into the physical world of sense perception and the development of individual consciousness are part of the history of humanity. In Egypt, we see the former manifesting itself in the enormous works of architecture. Tombs, which were grand affairs not at all like our cemeteries, were hewn from the solid rock. Temples of enormous proportions were built. The pyramids are still some of the world's wonders. The Sphinx still exists, demonstrating the dual nature of the human being.

The Egyptians considered the physical world to be a manifestation of the spiritual and, as their supersensible faculties receded, an attempt was made to understand the physical world by penetrating into its laws. Behind the phenomena lay spirit, so it was considered that penetration into the phenomena would lead to an understanding of the spirit. Thus, the Egyptian felt it necessary to make greater contact with external nature, and out of this impulse was born a sort of science which led to the study of medicine, mathematics, geometry, astrology and astronomy.

A further example of the penetration into matter is afforded by the development of the crafts—excellent examples of impressing mind on matter, and what could be a better illustration of coming to grips with material things than a banking system!

Considering again the matter of evolution in the sense of making closer contact with the physical world, we can gain some understanding of the strange procedure of mummification. The path of human development was into the physical world, but the desire to "escape" was apparently known in those days, as it is today. According to Rudolf Steiner, humanity would not have progressed had it not been for this mummification. People would have lost all interest in the physical world. By this means, attention was drawn to the physical body but, more essentially, the spirit of the deceased was, so to speak, fettered.

At death, the body normally disintegrates and the spirit severs this particular connection with earthly existence. If the body is preserved, the spirit is forced into a protracted relationship with the earth. From the spiritual world the soul is aware of the continuing existence of the body; thus its importance is magnified. Furthermore, as the spirits of the dead remained in close contact with the earth, it was easier for the initiates to contact them.

Mummification was also connected with the belief in eternal life. Eternal life was somehow connected with the preservation of the body and depended on it. It was thought that if the physical vehicle were preserved, it would not be the actual material that would rise again, but that the body itself would become spiritualized. It was, however, necessary to preserve its form.

For the Egyptian, the underworld was now an unknown, a world of peril. He was therefore given instruction on how life after death proceeds, and was taught that if a man uses his capacities on earth to further spiritual aims, he can be united with the spiritual powers after death. Instructions were given to the dead on how to get to heaven and these were inscribed on the walls of the tombs and on papyrus rolls which were buried with the bodies.

The soul had to undergo trials in the underworld. One of these was to come before the forty-two judges. Rudolf Steiner explains that these are really the ancestors and that the individual has to prove his worth to them. He has to show that he has advanced by cultivating what they left, i.e., he has had to cultivate his inheritance in the physical world. This is another significant pointer to the fact of closer connection with the physical world.

In the matter of the development of a greater consciousness of self, it is significant that the dead were buried with their possessions—weapons, clothing, ornaments. Even food offerings were made, as if life were to continue in the physical. Possessing things, a feeling of "this is mine," strengthens the ego. Being buried with possessions therefore greatly reinforced the consciousness of self to the still-living.

We mentioned earlier a religious revolution under Akhenaton. What really happened was that Akhenaton was aware of changes taking place in the manner of human perception and he himself experienced a "power within." What had been external was becoming an inner experience. It was the change from spiritual vision and guidance to inner activity—the change from the directive without to the directive within.

There is a parallel in Greek times where it is much more apparent. The Furies of the Greeks become the conscience of Socrates. In Akhenaton we find a first glimmer of this experience. In his beautiful hymn to Aton, the sun, we find expressed the idea that the sun or sun-god is also within: "Thou art in my heart." An extract from Prof. Breasted's translation follows:

When thou risest in the eastern horizon of heaven,
Thou fillest every land with thy beauty.

When thou settest in the western horizon of heaven,
The world is in darkness like the dead.

Bright is the earth when thou risest,
When thou shinest as Aton by day.
The darkness is banished when thou sendest forth thy rays.

How manifold are all thy works.
They are hidden from before us.
O thou sole God, whose powers no other possesseth.
Thou didst create the earth according to thy desire
While thou wast alone.

The world is in thy hand,
Even as thou hast made them.
When thou hast risen they live.
When thou settest they die.
For thou art duration beyond thy mere limbs.
By thee man liveth
And their eyes look upon thy beauty
Until thou settest.

Thou makest the beauty of form.
Thou art in my heart.

The Egyptians had many gods and, considering that we are dealing with a period of some two thousand years, and with a mixture of peoples, this is not surprising. However, the gods universally accepted were Osiris, Isis and Horus, and it is their story which gives the best characteristic of the significance of the Egyptian period. It is a mythical story, symbolic.

OSIRIS
Osiris was a good king, much concerned with the welfare of his people. He taught them the use of the plow, and the preparation of food. He built cities and gave instruction in the law, star wisdom and rhetoric. He travelled through the country teaching

these things and he also journeyed to other lands to do likewise. He was a peaceful ruler and sought to convert not by the sword, but by persuasion.

Osiris had a wicked brother called Seth (Typhon, by the Greeks) and a wife called Isis. Seth made a wonderful chest (secretly to Osiris' measurements) and, on the occasion of Osiris' return from one of his journeys, he gave a great feast and offered the chest to whomsoever it fitted. When Osiris lay down in it, the lid was shut fast and he was imprisoned. The chest with its contents was thrown into the Nile. It was eventually cast up on dry land and found by Isis who was searching for it.

In the meantime, Seth had made himself king. He learned that Isis had discovered the body and ordered it to be cut into fourteen pieces, each piece to be buried in a different place. Isis built a temple on the spot where each piece lay.

While Isis was wandering, a child, Horus, was born to her. He eventually drove Seth out and ruled in his place. Osiris became the king and judge of the dead.

This story symbolizes the historical development taking place—the withdrawing of the gods or, what is the same thing, the loss of direct clairvoyant vision. Osiris represents the eternal spiritual nature of humanity, the human soul and spirit in direct contact with the spiritual world. Material forces seek to imprison and destroy him. Although imprisoned and dissected, the spiritual forces still exist and a part of the human being (Isis) is aware of this. She seeks for the buried portions of the body and raises a temple over each part, i.e., erects a structure symbolizing the connection between spirit and matter. The temple is an outer manifestation of a spiritual reality. She bears a son, Horus, that is to say, new faculties are developed which can penetrate the world of matter with a different consciousness and find therein the spirit. So Horus drives out Seth and rules in his place. The spiritual world is the same as the world of the dead, hence Osiris has now become the king and ruler of the dead.

The story shows how the spiritual world has receded, but must be sought for in another dimension through the development of new human faculties. The death of Osiris is a picture of the disappearance of the old power of clairvoyance and the birth of Horus symbolizes the awakening of new forces. Isis represents a faculty still aware of the spiritual world. The famous inscription to Isis reads: "I am the All; I am the Past, the Present and the Future. No mortal can lift my veil." Mortal, in the Egyptian sense, means the human being whose perceptions are limited to the world of the senses. An "immortal" is one able to participate in supersensible experiences. The striving to be united with Osiris was the striving for the spiritual world.

In the parallel culture of Babylonia are to be found many aspects which are similar to those of Egypt. There is the same belief in gods and the same movement towards the physical world. The spiritual world is no longer immediately present, but must be attained. We see these things historically in both the beliefs and the legends.

Babylonia, together with Assyria, lay in the valleys of the Rivers Tigris and Euphrates. Like Egypt, the greater part of the area was flat and almost treeless. Like Egypt too, it was immensely fertile, and irrigation was practiced to grow large crops. Unlike Egypt, there were climatic seasons, a rainy one from November to March and a hot, dry summer. As there was no wood or stone in the plain, most of the buildings were of brick, and some magnificent palaces, temples and cities were built.

We hear much of Babylon in the Old Testament and possibly we become prejudiced, since the reading matter is presented from the Israelite point of view. Here we will try to look at the Babylonians from a more objective viewpoint.

That these peoples still felt themselves very much in contact with the spirit is seen in the fact that diseases were considered the work of demons which could be exorcised by means of incantations—somewhat similar to the Egyptian temple sleep. Poetry was the result of inspiration, and music was the imitation of the voices of the spirits. All culture still centered around the temple.

Their gods were Shamash, the sun-god, and Baal, the moon. Anu was Lord of the Sky and Destiny. Marduk (Merodach in the Old Testament) seems to have been a lesser deity although entitled King of the Gods. He it was who carried out the orders of Anu. Ea was known as the King of the Watery Deep, or Lord of the World—that means, of the world beneath, the earth. Spirits controlled all of nature and human lives.

Babylonian temples were the houses of the gods in a literal sense. The idols, or graven images, against which the Israelite prophets railed, were the physical bodies of the gods, and it was supposed that their spirits entered into the images. The statue was a manifestation. Hence, it was a devastating blow to the people when the enemy took away an idol. It was believed that the god himself had been taken prisoner and, as the god represented a sort of collective ego, the people were demoralized. The Romans were well aware of this when they took the conquered people's gods and put them in the Pantheon. However, the direction is toward the physical world and we see this in the stories of Ea, of Marduk, and in the development of social customs and a code of laws.

Ea was the River God, or the God of the Beneath. He was the artisan god who instructed the people how to make canals, grow crops, work metals, make pottery and bricks, build temples, form and use alphabetical signs and do mathematics. He gave a code of laws. We are reminded here of the Egyptian Osiris.

In the story of Marduk we have a picture of the receding clairvoyance and the development of senses attuned to the physical. Marduk is a sort of Michael figure. The gods appointed Marduk to fight the evil spirit called Tiamat, who had changed herself into a dragon. He rode forth in his chariot drawn by four war horses, armed with a thunderstone of lightning and with seven winds which he had created as helpers. The dragon opened her mouth seven miles wide to swallow him, but Marduk ordered six winds to blow down her mouth and the seventh to hold it open while he threw the thunderstone down her throat. The dragon was killed and Marduk then carved the body into two pieces, one half for the heavens, one half for the earth. He then created the sun and moon, the twelve groups of stars in the heavens, and plants, animals and human beings on earth.

Again, this is a symbolic story showing the change of consciousness. Tiamat, the dragon, is the world as it appears to one who has not developed the faculties of earthly sense perception, i.e., one who lives in a dream state, unable to differentiate between spirit and matter. With the development of earthly consciousness, the dragon is slain and the world appears in its physical manifestation. The thunderstone is the light of the intellect.

The trend towards the physical world is shown also in social customs and the setting up of a law, although these things only really come into their own with Rome. The Babylonians had courts and enforced laws. There were certain regulations concerning agriculture and irrigation. Taxes were portions of the produce but they were based on average yield. There were laws covering trespassing, animals, thieving and dishonesty. Service contracts were made for agricultural laborers. Physician's fees were payable according to rank.

A code of laws was set up by Hammurabi about the year 1940 BC. Hammurabi regarded himself not as the earthly ruler of all, but as a servant of the gods, and his laws were not so much between man and man (as established in Roman times), but sacred commandments received from Shamash, the sun-god. They have a religious background. They have a religious introduction and a religious ending. Demand is made for conscientious fulfillment as a duty to the gods. Non-fulfillment is a sin against the godhead.

It is also obvious from the laws that the person-to-person relationship has not yet developed, i.e., the feeling that every person is a separate individuality. This is evidenced in the provision for blood relatives to be punished for the crimes of their kin:

- If anyone strikes a pregnant woman and causes a miscarriage, there shall be a money payment. If the woman dies, the daughter of the person responsible shall be killed.

- If a house falls down and kills the owner's son, the builder's son shall be killed.

To our modern ideas of justice, this seems crude in the extreme, but we must bear in mind one of the basic themes of this dissertation—the development towards individuality. In those days, we have to think not of an individual ego, but of a group ego—hence, the whole family was involved.

The myths and stories of Babylonia give us further insight into the development which was then taking place. The story of Etana and, in particular, Gilgamesh, is very revealing. The former is very short and the latter somewhat complicated.

Etana was a king whose wife was expecting a child. He wished to learn the secrets of birth, and an eagle took him on its back through the seven starry regions where he learned what he wished to know.

The fact that the king wished to learn the secrets of birth shows the loss of spiritual vision. It is the same as wishing to learn the secrets of death. The eagle represents an intellectual force, and the journey through the starry regions is an obvious reference to some sort of initiation.

GILGAMESH

The Gilgamesh epic has come to us in several (incomplete) versions, and the rendering may therefore not be entire, but there is sufficient to make a good story which is a wonderful allegorical description. If the whole is too complicated, excerpts might be taken.

Gilgamesh was concerned with the problem of mortality, the search for knowledge, the escape from the common human fate. He appears as a tragic hero, striving, attaining and losing—an individual man battling with the odds in search of life and understanding.

Of the Pharaohs it was said that they were half god, half human. Of Gilgamesh it was said that he was two-thirds god, and one-third man. From his goddess mother he inherited beauty, strength and restlessness, from his father, mortality. He is engaged in the conflict between the divine and the earthly. We see the direction towards ego development in Gilgamesh's expressed desire "to leave on the earth an enduring name."

One of his dreams was interpreted as that destiny had given him kingship, but not eternal life. He was to "know" but not "experience" immortality (spiritual vision). The following is a very short outline of the story. The reader is recommended to study the full version of this epic.

THE EPIC OF GILGAMESH

Gilgamesh was the king of Uruk. He was a man who had tried to lead a full life, and had built great walls for the city and a temple, but this did not fulfill his ambitions. He could find no other outlets and became dissatisfied with life. Because of this, he became arrogant and selfish, and he lorded it over his people. The citizens, who resented this treatment, called on their god, Anu, for assistance, asking for his intervention. Anu, after due consideration with other gods, instructed Aruru, the goddess of creation, to make a being who would be the equal of Gilgamesh—a sort of second self. The idea was that the two would then contend with one another and leave the citizens in peace.

The goddess formed an image in her mind, dipped her hands in water and pinched off clay which she let fall in the wilderness. Thus was Enkidu (Eabani in other versions) created. The body of this newly formed being was rough and hairy. His food and drink were grass and water. He lived with the animals and had no communication with humankind.

One day, a hunter met him and was terrified by his appearance. The hunter ran back to his house and told his father of this strange creature. The father advised him to go to Gilgamesh, tell him about Enkidu, and ask that a woman be sent out who would entice the stranger into the city. The ruse succeeded. Enkidu was attracted to and seduced by the woman. After this, the animals rejected him. He was led by stages to wear clothes, to eat human food, to herd sheep, to make war on the wolf and the lion, and finally to enter the city. The woman described the strength and beauty of Gilgamesh to Enkidu, and told him of the way in which the king ruled his people. Enkidu's interest was aroused to such an extent that he decided to meet the king and challenge him. In the meantime, Gilgamesh had two dreams. In the first, he foresaw the coming of Enkidu and, in the second, he was told that the stranger would become a brave companion.

When Enkidu met the king in a wrestling match, he was thrown, recognized the master and the two became firm friends. Gilgamesh now wanted to go on a journey to the "Cedar Forest," or the "Country of the Living," to destroy the ferocious giant, Humbaba. Enkidu hesitated and entreated Gilgamesh to consult first with Shamash, the sun god, for the Cedar Forest was his. Gilgamesh prayed to Shamash for protection, but the god asked him the reason for his journey. In reply, Gilgamesh explained that he was tired of the city and wanted to go where no man's name was written, to set up a monument to the gods and to leave an "enduring name." Gilgamesh asks, "Why did you give me the desire for this adventure if it is not to be fulfilled?" Shamash is placated and promises assistance.

Gilgamesh's mother, seeing that he was determined to go on this dangerous quest, called Enkidu and asked him to protect her son. Then the two men set out. The story now contains a description of enormous distances covered, of mountains scaled, and of their arrival at the gate of the Cedar Forest. After breaking this down, they saw the Mountain of Cedars that was the dwelling place of the gods and the throne of Ishtar, the goddess of Uruk.

By now, they were tired and lay down to rest. Gilgamesh had a dream of a mountain falling down on him and being rescued by a blazing light. On a further occasion he had another dream. In this, the daylight disappeared, darkness fell among flashes of lightning and lowering of clouds; the fire went out and everything turned to ashes. Then he fell into a mysterious sleep.

Eventually, the two adventurers met Humbaba and the struggle began. Gilgamesh called on the god Shamash for assistance and Shamash sent "the great wind," the north wind, the whirlwind, the storm and the icy wind, the tempest and the scorching wind. They came like dragons, like a scorching fire, like a serpent that freezes the heart, a destroying flood and the lightning's fork. Humbaba was forced to yield and begged for his life. Gilgamesh was inclined to spare him, but not Enkidu. He insisted on his destruction and Humbaba was killed. The heroes returned home triumphantly.

The next incident in the story is the theft of Ishtar by a neighboring people. She was recaptured, however, by Gilgamesh, with the aid of Enkidu. On her return, Ishtar made advances to Gilgamesh, but he spurned her, and in revenge she asked the higher gods to send down the Bull of Heaven to lay waste the countryside of Uruk. The two friends attacked the bull and slew him.

Now Enkidu had a dream. He dreamed that the gods had held a council with one another and had decided "that because the two have killed Humbaba and the Bull of Heaven, one of them must die." Shamash claimed, however, that this was done at his request. Enkidu fell sick and died. The king was full of sorrow and lamented to his friend. "What is this sleep which holds you?" he asked. "You are lost in the dark and cannot hear me." Then Gilgamesh himself became sick and decided to undertake a journey to seek out Enkidu and his own healing. He had heard of one man who was immortal, his ancestor, Utnapishtim, and he was resolved to find him to learn the secrets of death and immortal life.

So Gilgamesh set out on a hazardous journey which took him through immense wildernesses, green pastures and over rugged mountains. He slew the lions guarding the mountain passes and came to the mountain which guards the rising and setting sun. At the gate of the mountain were two monsters, half men, half dragons, who were astounded that a mortal had penetrated to their domain. They explained that the passage through the mountain was twelve leagues of darkness, but Gilgamesh was undeterred, and they let him pass.

Gilgamesh made the journey through the blackness and arrived at the garden of the gods where he met Shamash himself.

Next he met a woman who barred his way, advising him to eat, drink and be merry. He explained who he was and the nature of his mission, and she then advised him to find the ferryman to take him across the water.

On the other side, he met Utnapishtim and explained that he had come to ask about the living and the dead. His chief quest was to find out how it was that Utnapishtim had achieved eternal life.

Utnapishtim told him the story of the flood and how the gods had granted him immortality because he knew their secret. However, for Gilgamesh and his generation, he said, things must be different. The times had changed and now all men must die. Nevertheless, Gilgamesh could acquire immortality if he could stay awake for six days and seven nights.

Gilgamesh decided to make the attempt but failed and fell asleep. Utnapishtim's wife gave him some magic food and he awoke refreshed. He was led to a fountain of healing where his sickness was cured and he was given clothes which would remain fresh until he reached home.

He was told of the existence of a magic plant which had the power of rejuvenation. This he obtained, but it was stolen from him by a serpent while he was bathing. He returned to his city, grieving for his friend and praying to the gods to restore him. Finally, the god of death allowed the ghost of Enkidu to appear and to answer questions concerning the netherworld.

In due course, Gilgamesh died and his people mourned him. They said of him that it was his destiny to be king, but it was not his destiny to achieve everlasting life.

To understand the Gilgamesh epic, it is necessary to remind ourselves again about the states of consciousness of peoples in the ancient civilizations. They did not see the physical world as we do today, but were aware of objects and events in supersensible worlds—a faculty which we have forfeited for our material concepts.

There was no sharp division between the physical and spiritual world. Hence, there was no death as we understand it. The spirit passed from the body but was still perceptible. Since there was no death, there was everlasting life or, if we use a modern term, a continuity of consciousness. Thus the search for the secret of death and the search for everlasting life can be equated. In a time when consciousness of the spiritual world was receding in favor of greater awareness of the physical, the search for everlasting life becomes the search for entry to the spiritual world.

Gilgamesh lived in such a period when the physical world was becoming the greater reality, when the old clairvoyant powers were fading and when, in addition, a feeling of egohood, at least among the leaders of civilization, was beginning to be felt. This is pictured in the building of the walls, the temple, in dissatisfaction with life, selfishness and lording it over his people. Like Faust, Gilgamesh was searching, but he lived in the actual age of the twilight of the gods; that is, he was living in both spiritual and physical worlds, but with the consciousness of the spiritual receding. His dreams also point to this fact.

The citizens, still within the old consciousness, called upon Anu, the father of the gods, for assistance. He consulted with the other deities and Enkidu is created. Enkidu could be looked upon as representative of that portion of the human soul which remembers its connection with the divine or as representing ancient clairvoyance. In the story, Enkidu is seduced by a woman, then the animals reject him. He wears clothes, eats human food and finally comes to the city. This is a picture of the dimming of clairvoyant vision and entry into the physical world.

Enkidu is brought to Gilgamesh and the two contend, then become friends, i.e., Gilgamesh experiences a reawakening of spiritual perception, but of the old type. Gilgamesh wants to go on a journey to the "Cedar Forest," or the "Country of the Living," to destroy the ferocious giant, Humbaba, and to leave "an enduring name."

Gilgamesh represents the forward evolutionary development of the human being, and we can think of this journey as something taking place in the soul world. He wishes to make progress in his own development, under his own impetus. To leave "an enduring name" means that he is seeking to become more united with the physical world.

This adventure is a dragon-slaying episode. There are forces in one's own being which must be overcome in order to progress. Enkidu—the old power—is nervous and does not want to go. He probably senses that he is doomed. Gilgamesh manifests his progressive nature towards egohood by asserting that he must leave a record of himself in earthly success. Enkidu suggests that

Gilgamesh should first consult Shamash, the sun-god, for the Cedar Forest belongs to him. Here we have an obvious indication of a spiritual realm and the fact that one should seek spiritual guidance. The question that Gilgamesh puts shows the direction of his development. He asks of Shamash, "Why did you give me the desire for this adventure if it is not to be fulfilled?" It is the cry of a man seeking to know his own nature and destiny—a man who is no longer being divinely led. He explains that he is tired of the city and wants to go where no man's name is written to set up a monument to the gods, i.e., he is tired of the physical world and is seeking the spiritual.

Shamash grants him special assistance in the form of the winds—a picture of spiritual help. Special weapons are made—a picture of soul development. The description of the journey, the dreams and events, are soul experiences. The mysterious sleep means a dimming of the consciousness. In the struggle with Humbaba, Gilgamesh is inclined to spare him, i.e., he is almost deceived by evil, or not sufficiently awake to recognize its real nature, but Enkidu urges him to complete the destruction. It is like the story of Hansel and Gretel, where Gretel, the soul force, suddenly recognizes the old witch for what she is. The knowledge suddenly dawns and Humbaba, like the witch, is destroyed.

Then the city of Uruk is attacked by enemies and the goddess Ishtar is stolen. The significance of this can only be understood if we remember that the older peoples were lacking in a feeling of individuality. They lived in tribes or communities and had, as it were, a group soul, or a group ego. The goddess Ishtar represents this. Thus, when she is stolen, it is like human beings losing their egos—the citizens were demoralized and lost their spiritual direction.

One might also say that Ishtar's disappearance is another picture of the receding spiritual world. With Enkidu's help, Gilgamesh recovers the goddess, i.e., again the clairvoyant faculty is reawakened in him.

Now the goddess makes advances to the king and he rejects her. He realizes now that there are dangers in making this connection with the spiritual world—he would lose his individuality in the group consciousness. He retrieved Ishtar with the help of Enkidu (the old clairvoyance), and this is no longer the path to supersensible realms. The strength of a growing individuality is portrayed in the temerity with which he speaks to the goddess when rejecting her. His invective is quite entertaining. He calls her:

A brazier which smolders in the cold.
A back door which keeps out neither wind nor storm;
A castle which crushes the garrison;
Pitch that blackens the bearer.
A leaky skin that wets the carrier.
A sandal that trips the wearer.

Ishtar calls on the gods to send down the Bull of Heaven to avenge her. Gilgamesh and Enkidu do battle with the bull and slay it. In the story of the Bull of Heaven, we have a picture of time events. It is the transition from one civilization to another, a transition from one state of mind to another. The Egypto-Chaldean-Babylonian epoch stood under the cosmic influence of Taurus, the Bull. The slaying of the bull denotes the change into another period during which a new form of consciousness was to be developed. So Shamash claims that the bull's death was at his request, i.e., in the divine plan. Enkidu falls sick and dies—that is, the old form of atavistic clairvoyance dies out. Gilgamesh laments. His friend has gone and he knows not whither. He too becomes sick. It is the sickness of mortality. With the loss of spiritual vision, he has become conscious that man is mortal. Death, mortality, loss of spiritual vision, these are one and the same thing. He now has to seek spiritual knowledge through initiation by his own efforts. So he decides on a journey to seek his ancestor Utnapishtim to find out the secrets of death, of everlasting life, or to experience the spiritual world—all of which have the same significance.

Again, the physical events described in the journey can only be understood as soul experiences—the monsters, the lion, the endless blackness, the garden of the gods, the temptation to give up. Significantly, in the garden of the gods he meets the sun-god himself, i.e., he is aware of the divine presence in a state of consciousness different from the one he had in the Cedar Forest where he had slept and dreamed.

He crosses the ocean and finds Utnapishtim. When the latter explains his immortality, he is really explaining that he, having lived in antediluvian times, had had a natural spiritual insight and that, therefore, there was for him no death. The crossing of the threshold for him and his contemporaries did not entail a change of consciousness. "Now," says Utnapishtim, "all men must die," meaning that in the new age human beings will be aware of a spiritual and physical world, but will be without insight into the spiritual. Gilgamesh can achieve immortality (spiritual vision) only by staying awake (in the spirit). He is at the portal of initiation. He falls asleep, however, and therefore the secrets of the spiritual world are not revealed to him. The door is closed. Nevertheless, his sojourn in the realm beyond refreshes him, like sleep. He obtains the magic plant of rejuvenation but loses it again, i.e., he cannot tap the real source of life.

When he returns to his city, he is conscious of the existence of a spiritual world which he has entered, and which now manifests itself to him vicariously (Enkidu's appearance), but in which he is not at home. It is almost as if he had, as it were, learned the alphabet, but not learned to read the book.

Thus, in this story we have a picture which shows the loss of direct original clairvoyance. The golden age has passed. Gilgamesh seeks to attain direct knowledge of the spiritual world through initiation but does not succeed.

In the next cultural epoch, Greece and Rome, we shall see how further progress is made towards individualism and the material world.

The Fourth Cultural Epoch

As in the case of the earlier cultural epochs, it is not the aim here to give a complete history of the period, but to deal with the essential and special characteristics of these civilizations in the context of the whole of the history teaching. At the same time, we must bear in mind the age of the children concerned. At a later stage in the school, when pupils have reached the age of sixteen or seventeen, it is possible to deal with the historical developments and their significance more thoroughly. At present, we are dealing with children of eleven and twelve, to whom we want to convey the essence of the Graeco-Roman period.

In eleven-year-old children the intellectual faculties are only just awakening. We must therefore still give scope to the feeling-imaginative understanding; i.e., we give stories and background information in a descriptive manner, although it is now also possible to introduce a few concepts.

Our general theme in teaching history is the development and evolution of the human being. It traces the development of humanity from the time when we were conscious of a spiritual world but had little self-consciousness, to a time of awareness of the material world only, and a strong consciousness of self as an individual with growing powers of thinking.

The Graeco-Roman period shows:

- The further conquest of the physical world
- The development of individuality
- The birth of thinking

These things, however, manifest themselves differently in different civilizations. We must therefore treat them separately. The task is especially complicated since there is such an abundance of material and, in the setting of the school, not much time available. In the Steiner school curriculum perhaps two or three weeks can be devoted to Greece in Class Five (age eleven), and four weeks in Class Six to Rome. It is possible, however, to bring some of the material into other lessons. There is no reason, for instance, why some of the literature should not be used as a reader. The stories from Greece can be told over the whole year in Class Five, and those of Rome in Class Six. In using the suggestions made here, the teacher should not be deflected from finding and making use of any other material which may appeal to him or her.

It is always advantageous in teaching children to connect their minds to something they already know. Since history is not an isolated series of events, this aspect is particularly important. If pupils find things of Greek or Roman origin about them, their interest is stimulated. In this case, there is no great difficulty since there are immediate examples in the language we speak. A great many of our learned and scientific words come from the Greek or Latin, and we should find that a great many common words are Latin if we were to pursue their derivation. Words such as *philosophy, biology, metamorphosis, photograph, telescope, telephone* are Greek. From the Latin come such expressions as *intelligent, judiciary, domicile, conduct, transfer, library*. Ideas and systems of organization have been bequeathed to us, for instance, democratic government and the hierarchical church system. In England are many physical reminders of the Roman presence which we will mention later. If we travel into the Mediterranean, we find both Greek and Roman remains.

After some sort of general introduction describing the land, peoples, customs and beliefs, there are four main themes which must be dealt with. The first is the mythology or, rather, the stories from the mythologies. These can be told or read simply as stories during the whole year. The second and third themes touch upon the internal political development and the external historical events. The fourth is biography, due to the fact that outstanding personalities now appear—human, in contrast to divinely inspired personalities—and we must therefore give biographies. In actual practice the themes may interweave.

Greece

As with India, Persia and Egypt, it is interesting to look at the geographical structure of the country whose civilization we are about to describe, and the way it came to be settled.

Greece presents a stark contrast to Egypt. It is very mountainous, with an extraordinarily jagged coastline. It consists of land which was once submerged but was thrust up through volcanic activity. Off the coast are over five hundred islands. The scenery is varied; sometimes it offers bare landscape, sometimes snow-capped mountains. There are grasslands and forests. On the coastal plains and in the lower valleys, crops such as corn, vines, olives and oranges can be grown. Metals are found in the mountains. Much of the rock is marble, hence a beautiful building material is at hand. There is a great deal of sunshine.

In its heyday, Greece was at the crossroads of the world. To the east was Asia Minor, to the south, Egypt and North Africa; to the north were the Alps and, in the west, the Pillars of Hercules (Gibraltar). Beyond these bounds the world was unknown or, rather, to the Greek mind, there was no world beyond.

Ancient Greece was settled by tribes which came from the north and the east—the Ionians, Achaeans, Aeolians, Dorians, etc. The terrain made communications difficult and, although related, these peoples did not become one nation but organized themselves into the so-called city-states. They spent a great deal of time fighting one another but, at the same time, they felt united in many ways. They spoke the same language; they shared the same ideas about the gods and the evolution of the world. They had similar ideas on government. Their athletes met together every four years for the Olympic games when contests were held in running, jumping, wrestling, discus and javelin throwing.

The Greeks spoke of gods, titans and heroes. These were, in varying degrees, supernatural beings. The titans were the children of earth and heaven, created by powerful gods in the past, and presently ruling gods like Zeus were their descendants. The heroes were half gods and half mortals. (We would call them initiates.)

The gods lived on Mount Olympus. A gate of clouds, kept by goddesses called the Seasons, used to open and shut to let them in and out. Zeus was the chief ruler and Aphrodite, the goddess of beauty. Phoebus Apollo was the god of the sun and the most beautiful. Music, poetry and the fine arts were under his care. Artemis was the goddess of the moon and of the hunt; Athene, the goddess of wisdom; Poseidon, the god of the sea. Eros was the god of love, and Hades, of the underworld. The gods were ever-present to the Greeks, who believed that they helped them and intervened in their affairs.

There were also nature spirits who lived in the trees, woods and rivers. Naiads were the nymphs of the brooks, streams and lakes. Dryads lived in the trees; Satyrs, in the woods and fields. Aeolus was the king of the winds, which he kept shut up in a cave, letting them out occasionally.

The Greeks had two special institutions which we find difficult to understand. One was the so-called Mystery Center, and the other the Oracle. The mystery centers were really places of learning. They were a sort of church and university combined, but the scholars in them learned to appreciate and perceive spiritual forces behind the world of matter. The oracles were a sort of temple, or were situated in the temples. If anyone had a problem, he could bring it to the priest at the oracle who was conditioned to hear the voices of the gods. Through the priest the suppliant would get an answer.

From the above information, it will be obvious that the Greeks were in some measure still in touch with the spiritual world. In addition, there is much factual information which can be given, as, for instance, the Greek way of living—interests, foods, clothing, houses, etc., not forgetting their great achievements in drama, architecture and sculpture, but this is readily available in history books or textbooks and is not included here.

THE GREEK STORIES

We have already mentioned the birth of philosophy in Greece about the year 600 BC. A new means of perception was developing in the human mind. The old faculty of spiritual vision or clairvoyance was disappearing and thinking was taking its place. The direction was towards intellectual thinking and secular life. The Greek of that time felt himself in something of a half world. He felt some connection with a spiritual world but was losing consciousness of it.

The stories and legends of Greece arise out of this twilight of the mind. They are representations of real happenings or experiences. They are symbolic, allegorical. For this reason they are also particularly suitable for children of the eleven/twelve age group. The stories mirror the pupils' own development since they too are emerging from a more dreamlike state into one of clearer consciousness. This objective picture of their own development serves to give them a hold in life as they are given a picture of their own experience. For the children themselves, it is enough to tell the stories and no background information should be given at this stage. They may well look at these things again with a different understanding in Classes Ten and Eleven. It is, however, useful for the teacher to penetrate a little more closely into the significance of the material.

Five stories may well be used as class readers in Class Five, or for silent reading, or the teacher can digest them first and retell them. It is worth mentioning that a story works much more powerfully if it is told rather than read. This is the material which can be spread over the year and need not necessarily be compressed into the main lesson's three- or four-week period. Indeed, this would hardly be possible.

The five stories are: *The Iliad, The Odyssey, The Argonauts, Theseus* and *Perseus.* The first two deal with the Trojan War and its aftermath, and are available in many shortened forms. The originals are rather formidable. The other three are contained in Charles Kingsley's delightful book, *The Heroes*. It is not necessary to give the content of these stories here, only to draw attention to their significance.

THE ILIAD

In *The Iliad* we have the story of the Greek heroes who had sailed to Troy (or Ilium) to rescue Helen, the wife of Menelaus, King of Sparta. She had been abducted by Paris, a son of Priam, King of Troy. Whatever the historical merits of the story, we observe several matters relative to the general historical theme.

Comparing the *Mahabharata* with the Iliad, we notice quite different ideas and attitudes. In the former, there come to expression ideas of noble courage rising above the fear of death, of generosity, princely behavior, honor, hatred of killing and forgiveness of enemies. A lofty spiritual tradition is apparent. In the Iliad, we find expressions of fear, hatred, anger, jealousy, fraud, cruelty, lust to kill. In other words, the Iliad shows a much more modern aspect. The self-responsible individual is emerging and his lower nature manifests itself.

The war between the Greeks and the Trojans is a war between men who are directed by the gods, yet there is a difference between the adversaries. In the Orient, to which Troy belonged, there were priests and monarchs divinely inspired who directed the masses. Thus, we see in Troy an ancient patriarchal civilization headed by Priam, who was both king and priest, surrounded by his fifty sons and daughters. The chief characters have an air of nobility.

By contrast, the Greeks are sharply characterized individuals, with very human reactions. Achilles is furious, Odysseus, wily. Agamemnon has lust for power. The Greeks are away from home, in a foreign land. "Homelessness" in a story can very often be interpreted as a seeking for something new. The struggle between the Trojans and the Greeks is a struggle between the old and the new. On the one hand, there are priest-dominated masses and, on the other, individuals. (We shall see the same sort of struggle in the Persian wars with the Greeks). The contest is between theocracy and democracy, clairvoyant consciousness and independent thinking. The end of the story is significant.

Troy is overcome by the ruse of the wooden horse—by thinking human cleverness dependent on the intellect, which wins the day. For the Greeks, this saga was something more than a story or history. It showed them the essential difference between themselves and the peoples who were still living in the old consciousness.

THE ODYSSEY

The sequel to *The Iliad* is *The Odyssey*, the wanderings of Odysseus. This is possibly the most important story of all for our particular purpose. If all else were sacrificed, this story alone would give some idea of the Greek mission.

Odysseus leaves Troy with his companions on his return journey to Greece. He is wind- and storm-tossed, loses all his friends, endures innumerable hardships, returns home penniless and an outcast, to find his wife being wooed by others who would like to marry her and take over the kingdom.

The story may be based upon fact but it is on quite another plane that we can understand it. We can look upon it as an allegory and transfer the events to the experiences and strivings of the developing human being.

Odysseus overcomes the Cyclops, the one-eyed monster. The single eye represents the old form of consciousness. This is destroyed. A monster usually portrays the forces of the lower nature, the purely physical. Odysseus recognizes Circe as an evil being and has some mystical experience, as evidenced by his descent to the nether world. He withstands the blandishments of the Sirens (worldly attractions). He sails between Scylla and Charybdis (he keeps a balance between two opposing negative forces). He spends seven years with Calypso. This is a picture of a man in search of his own soul. He stays with Alcinous; he appreciates the joys of the world. He gets home, shipwrecked and in rags. The significance is that he has lost everything of a transitory nature but he has found himself. He is "home," and he becomes "master in his own house." Athene has been his special guide and friend. In other words, he has been guided by the power of clear thought.

Odysseus has advanced from the natural clairvoyant state. He has attained greater consciousness and a mastery over the lower emotions. He has trod the path of individual responsibili-

ty. He has used his "head." To be "master in one's own house"
means to be master of oneself, to rule the emotions by thought,
and to be conscious of oneself as an independent individuality.
The Odyssey demonstrates the special mission of the Greek in picture form. We shall see the same thing in different guise when we
consider the development of philosophy.

THE ARGONAUTS

The story of the Argonauts shows the change in consciousness
between one cultural epoch and another. Phryxos and Helle were
twins who were suffering from the cruelty of their stepmother.
They were advised to flee, and were transported eastwards on
the back of a ram with a golden fleece. Helle fell into the water
(hence the name Hellespont), but Phryxos reached Colchis where
the ram was sacrificed and its fleece given to the king of that
country. The king hung it on an oak tree where it was guarded by
a fierce dragon. Jason, together with the help of Medea, the king's
daughter, recovered it. First, he had to overcome two fire-breath-
ing bulls, then plow land with them and sow dragons' teeth, from
which immediately sprang armed warriors. Then he had to overcome the dragon. In these exploits he was successful, and he
sailed back home with the golden fleece.

The interpretation of this story is something like this: the
stepmother represents the enclosing forces of the material world,
the fading of spiritual vision. (There is the same theme in fairy
stories such as "Hansel and Gretel"; it is the stepmother who
causes the children to be cast out of their father's house.) Direct
vision was the possession of the eastern peoples, and this vision
was a combination of knowledge and religion. This sort of wisdom still existed in the east, and the golden fleece represents this.
But in the west, in Greece, the old faculties were dying out and
new ones were taking their place. It was only possible in Greece
to obtain this type of knowledge through a process of initiation,
and initiation requires trials and a strengthening of self. The
Argonauts are the initiates. In order to obtain the golden fleece,
Jason must overcome his lower passions, which he does with the
help of Medea, his higher self. (We have already seen similar
processes in the cases of Zarathustra and Gilgamesh.) The heroes
bring back the fleece to Greece. That is to say, the mystery schools
are founded where pupils, by a process of initiation, may acquire

the wisdom which humanity of earlier times had possessed naturally.

This story, of course, refers to the beginning of Greek culture. It was the task of the Greeks to develop the power of thinking, and during the course of their civilization, the mystery schools were superseded. We shall return to this point when we discuss Socrates.

THESEUS

Theseus is the hero who slays a bull-like monster, the Minotaur, to whom human sacrifice had to be made. To find this creature, he has to penetrate to the center of a labyrinth and then find his way out again. He is able to do this by means of a thread given to him by the princess, Ariadne.

In the world cycle of events, there is a change of civilization approximately every two thousand years. This figure coincides with a twelfth part of the cosmic year. The cosmic or Platonic year lasts for 25,920 earth years. There are twelve signs of the Zodiac, hence each cultural epoch takes place under the influence of one particular sign. The Egypto-Chaldean civilization developed under Taurus, the bull, hence the frequent reference to bull themes. When the Taurus period ended, Aries, the ram, became the dominating influence. This sign denotes intellect.

Theseus kills the Minotaur. This represents the end of the Taurus period and the beginning of that of Aries, in which the intellect is the important factor. The monster is overthrown by using Ariadne's thread—logical thought. The labyrinth can be thought of as the human brain. As with so many of these stories, there may be a factual basis, as well as a symbolical one. Indeed, they may be understood on many different levels.

Another interpretation of the Theseus adventure would be to think of man struggling with his own lower nature. At first, he loses. This is the human sacrifice—his good impulses are destroyed. Then his better self, the princess, emerges, and using brains and intelligence—the thread—he wins through.

PERSEUS

Perseus is one on whom the gods shower favors. He is inspired by Athene and given winged sandals by Mercury. He slays

Medusa, the Gorgon with snakes for hair. He then overcomes a dragon and rescues his bride-to-be. This theme is found in all mythologies and fairy tales. The human being overcomes evil through the forces given to him by the gods. Finding his bride is like the prince finding the princess, i.e., his true self. In this particular case, the assistance is given by Athene, that is, by using the power of thought.

We will now consider some of the shorter stories which can be used within the actual three- or four-week history period.

DEMETER AND PERSEPHONE

The drama of Demeter and Persephone typifies what was happening within the soul of the individual Greek. This story is usually interpreted as the story of springtime, but its real significance lies much deeper. Demeter, or Ceres, is the earth-mother whose daughter has been abducted by Hades (Pluto), king of the underworld. By divine decree, the girl shall be released if she has not eaten while in the underworld. She has, however, partaken of six pomegranate seeds, and hence it is decided that for six months she must live in the lower world and for six months in the upper.

To the Greeks, nature was something more than plants and landscapes. Nature was the great all-sustaining, all-pervading power and was experienced as a living being known as Demeter. In our modern, abstract way of thinking, we would say that Demeter represents the immortal or the spiritual world. The human soul, born of the divine, incarnates. Thus, we see Persephone seized by Hades, and her vision of the earth, sea and sky disappear. This means that the memory of the divine is lost, and the figures that Persephone now sees about her appear as ghosts. They are the physical beings, but appear only as shadows because their spiritual counterpart is no longer visible. The significance of eating means that the senses become bound to the lower world. Henceforth, the human soul is a citizen of two separate worlds. Eventually, though this is not contained in the story, the experience of the spiritual world fades entirely.

HERCULES

Hercules is a figure who always excites interest. From what we have already said in several connections, it will be apparent to the reader now what his twelve labors really represent. Again, we have a path of initiation. The labors are really the path of the inner development of the soul. In overcoming the beasts, Hercules is controlling his own lower desires. In cleansing the Augean stables, he is purifying his own soul. Obtaining the apples of the Hesperides means that he gains immortality. In this connection, as with Gilgamesh, it is the same thing as spiritual vision. With this knowledge, he was able to visit the kingdom of Hades and subdue Cerberus, that is, he solved the mystery of death.

PROMETHEUS

The epic of Prometheus embraces a wider epoch than Greece itself. Let us recall for a moment the general theme of our whole history teaching, which is to show how human beings gain a greater awareness of the physical world, and at the same time, a greater consciousness of themselves as individuals. We have characterized this development in the earlier epochs. In Greek times there was a definite turning point.

The Prometheus saga symbolizes a development which began long before Greek times and will continue long after. At the same time, it vividly characterized the change. We said that the Graeco-Roman period shows a further entanglement with the physical world, a growing feeling of personality, and a switch to the use of individual intelligence. These matters are incorporated in the Prometheus story.

Prometheus is the legendary creator of the human being and giver of talents. He steals fire from the gods and gives it to humanity. For this, he pays the price. He is chained to a rock, and a vulture gnaws at his liver during the day; it grows again during the night. He has a secret which Zeus would like to know, but he does not reveal it until he is rescued by Hercules. Chiron, the Centaur, is sacrificed in his place.

Prometheus represents that supernatural power which guides humanity towards the physical. When the story speaks of the creation of the human being, we must think of creation in the physical sense. The human being was in existence in a spiritual form before becoming clothed with a physical body. It is a matter of immortality putting on mortality. The human spirit, having incarnated in a physical body, now turns its attention towards the conquest of the physical world, or rather, it is directed towards this world. Hence Prometheus is described as the agency which teaches humanity to write, to build ships, to use wood, stone and metals, but above all, he gives the fire of the gods to the human being, and the latter acquires intelligence, the power of thinking. This makes humans the potential equal of the gods. (In another story from another culture, we are told that the human being ate of the tree of knowledge.) Prometheus himself is now chained to a rock, which represents the physical world, and he endures great suffering. He knows a secret, but will only divulge it when the time is ripe. He knows that Zeus must marry a mortal to produce a son who will be god-like; that is to say that the divine must unite with the human to produce human wisdom. It could be expressed another way: original spiritual vision is lost to mortal man, but through the use of the divine fire, the power of thinking, to penetrate the physical world, the human consciousness is reawakened to the existence and perception of the spiritual in a new form. This can only happen at a certain point in evolution.

Hercules is the one who achieves this spiritual development. He becomes an initiate and has the power to overcome the evil that threatens Prometheus. The Centaur, half man and half animal, is sacrificed in his place. The lower instincts are overcome. Teachers will find the following poem useful (dactylic hexameter):

Hymn to Prometheus

Hail to Prometheus, the Titan, the helper of man and creator.
Clay was the substance he used and in likeness of gods then he shaped it.
Goodness and evil from hearts of the beasts in man's breast he enfolded.
Fire he brought down from the realms of the skies to perfect his creation.
Movements of stars he explained to the wondering earth-dwelling people.
Numbers he taught them to use and the plants which heal sickness he showed them.
Symbols he taught them to write, representing the sounds of their speaking.
Building of ships he did teach, and the training of beasts to man's service.
Into the depths of the earth did he guide men to find precious metals.
Zeus he defied and brought fire down again when the god would deny men.
Torment and anguish he suffered for harsh was the fate decreed for him.
Bound to a cliff and tormented and tortured by day by a vulture.
Bravely the Titan endured and at length one arrived to release him.

These are the stories and legends which we consider best suited for this particular period of history. Naturally, a teacher may have a special liking for others and should use them. There are many shorter stories which should be read or told to the children. Many of them illustrate the feeling of the Greeks for the divine in nature.

Next, we will consider the political developments.

THE GREEK CITY-STATES

Not until the time of Philip of Macedonia and Alexander the Great did the Greeks become one nation. Originally, they organized themselves into city-states that, by modern standards, were relatively small. A state had perhaps a population of some hundred thousand inhabitants and was about the size of an average English county. The states were often at war with one another.

Although they spoke the same language, had the same ideas, and although the same development towards a feeling of individuality was taking place in all of them, each citizen was very conscious of the community in which he lived. The personal became manifest in the artistic-philosophical sphere; in social and political matters it was restricted by community consciousness.

Nevertheless, it was the Greeks who gave us the word *democracy*, rule by the people, and the Greek states were organized as democracies. Two of the most famous were Athens and Sparta, sometimes rivals and sometimes allies, presenting a great contrast in some respects and great similarities in others.

Solon was the great lawgiver of Athens. He lived from 638 to 558 BC, and was a wealthy merchant, philosopher, poet and traveller. Disagreements and divisions of parties had created chaos, and it was Solon who remodelled the constitution. Among other things, it was decided that: all those who were in prison for debt should be freed; no man should be made a slave for debt; all classes of people should have a voice in the affairs of state; men of every class should serve as jurymen in courts of law; a senate of four hundred members was created. Solon improved the coinage and introduced a better scale of weights and measures. In the course of time, Athens became the leading city in the artistic and intellectual field.

Sparta had been given its laws somewhat earlier by Lycurgus, who lived in the ninth century BC. Sparta was the capital city of the district known as Laconia. Lycurgus, like Solon, had been a great traveller. He had visited Crete, Egypt, India, and had studied their laws, government and customs. As a state of anarchy was prevailing in Sparta at the time, the people asked Lycurgus to draw up new laws. This he did.

The highest position in the state was to be occupied by two kings, and their powers were counterbalanced by a senate of twenty-eight persons. The kings only ruled by popular will. They were more figureheads than rulers. They had the privilege of giving their opinions first in the assemblies, acted as umpires in disputes and commanded the army. There was a national assembly to which elected representatives were sent from the other cities of Laconia. Thus, the people had a say in public affairs.

Lycurgus requisitioned all the land, which was then parcelled out again equally. Customs were introduced to condition the boys for hardship, with the idea of producing good soldiers. At seven, boys left their mothers and were trained in arms and feats of endurance. They went barefoot and naked in the summer and had only a simple cloak in winter. They slept on reeds gathered by their own hands. They were flogged to toughen them. Whereas Athens cultivated the artistic, Sparta devoted itself to war. The city had no walls. The boast was that its soldiers were its walls. Talking was discouraged—hence our word *laconic*.

Legend has it that Lycurgus wanted to ask the oracle at Delphi if his laws were good. Before he went, he assembled the citizens and extracted an oath from them to respect his laws at least until he returned. He then journeyed to Delphi, and the oracle pronounced his laws: "Perfect! As long as Sparta observes them, she will surpass all other cities in glory." He sent this message home and starved himself to death.

The Spartan attitude is well illustrated in the story of Leonidas and his three hundred men. With allies, they were holding the pass of Thermopylae against the Persian army, but a traitor showed the invaders a way around. The Spartan law said, "Conquer or die." Leonidas and his soldiers fought to the last man and all died. A stone with these words now marks the spot where they fell with the words:

Go, wayfarer, to Sparta.
Say that here, obeying her, we fell.

Another little anecdote tells of a Spartan who was asked how he became so famous. His answer was: "By despising death." There is also the story of a mother waiting at the city gates for news of a battle in which her six sons were fighting. A messenger came and she was told that five were killed. "That was not what I wanted to know," she said. "How did the battle go?"

"We were victorious," was the reply.

"Then I am satisfied," she answered.

We see then in the city-states the beginnings of democracy. All men were citizens and played an active part. The single citizen identified himself with the corporate life. Let us quote Pericles:

> Our constitution is called a democracy because power is in the hands not of a minority, but of the whole people. When it is a question of settling private disputes, everyone is equal before the law. . . . No-one is kept in political obscurity by his poverty. . . . Our love of what is beautiful does not lead to extravagance; our love of the things of the mind does not make us soft.

Yet the above statement has to be qualified. Women played little part in public affairs, and not all men took full part. Greek culture flourished on the basis of slavery, but the attitude to slaves was on the whole a benevolent one. A great many slaves were prisoners of war. To the Greeks, it seemed that some people were born to rule and others to serve. What mattered was that all should be incorporated in a well-ordered society which functioned harmoniously.

EXTERNAL HISTORY

As far as we are concerned here, the main historical events center around the war with Persia. Whatever may be given in detail, the main point is the clash between east and west—despotism versus democracy.

There were some Greek settlements in Asia Minor, a part of the Persian Empire, and they revolted against their overlords. Athens sent help, and Darius, the Persian ruler, decided to punish the city and subjugate all Greece. He transported an enormous army by sea in 490 BC and landed a little north of Athens at Marathon.

The Athenians now sent a swift runner to Sparta, their greatest rival, to ask for help. He covered the distance of over a hundred miles of broken country in less than two days. The Spartan force reached Athens in three days, only to find that battle had already been joined, and the Persians defeated. Some ten thousand Greek soldiers had been involved and they had been heavily outnumbered. One estimate of Persian dead alone was six thousand. The Persian fleet returned to Asia.

Darius died in 485 BC and was succeeded by Xerxes, who decided to add Greece to his empire. He built a bridge of boats to cross the Hellespont, but this was destroyed in a storm. A second bridge was built and, according to reports, it took seven days and nights for the Persian hosts to cross. The army consisted of men from all quarters of the Persian empire. It is said that there were so many that the rivers of Greece were exhausted, so many men took water from them. The numbers involved are estimated at three hundred thousand. They came through the pass of Thermopylae after overcoming the resistance there.

While the armies were crossing the land, a Persian supply fleet was sailing towards Athens. The city was abandoned, but the oracle had prophesied that it would be given impregnable walls of wood. This is taken as a reference to the Greek ships which sailed out to meet the enemy.

In the great naval battle of Salamis, 480 BC, the Persians were defeated. The following year, they were defeated again in another sea battle at Samos, and on land at Plataea. In 468 BC, on the banks of the river Eurymedon, the Greeks won another great victory, and the Persian might was broken for all time. Xerxes was murdered in 465 BC, and his empire disintegrated.

The Greek-Persian war was a struggle between individuals and dictatorship. The Greeks were learning that all should have a say in making laws which all would obey because they were agreed on by popular will. The east was still ruled by despots. The point is well illustrated in a report that Thucydides made on a conversation between the Persian king and some Greek prisoners. The Greeks say that they fight as free men and of their own volition, but the Persians cannot believe them.

BIOGRAPHIES

(These are only short notes. The teacher is recommended to make a more detailed study of those characters that interest him or her.)

We have spoken of Greek times as the time of the birth of the personality and of independent thinking. Children of eleven are becoming more aware of themselves as individualities and, therefore, from both points of view it is right and proper now to deal with personalities in a biographical manner. Naturally, in speaking about individualities much will also be contributed to a general appreciation of the whole period of culture. There are a great many characters the description of which would be extremely useful. Those taken will depend to some extent on the teacher's taste and the time available, but children should know something of those suggested.

Although of undoubted interest, it is not necessary to deal with all details of their lives. We must bring out the salient points relative to our studies. It is a matter of characterization, of bringing home the fact that there are individualities, that we distinguish separate and distinct personalities. It is not necessary to say this in so many words. The very fact that one describes these persons has its own subtle effect.

PYTHAGORAS (584-506 BC)

When Pythagoras is mentioned, most of us think of the theorem which bears his name. Neglecting the rest of his biography is one of the great sins committed against us in our education. Pythagoras was a great scholar with universal knowledge, who wanted to understand the world rationally. The oracle at Delphi had promised his mother "a son who would be useful to all people and throughout all time." He was a great searcher for knowledge and sought this from priests and philosophers. He found contradictions in their teachings, but was content to absorb their wisdom and to meditate upon it. He realized that earth, heaven and humanity are all interconnected, and that there are common rhythms in the human being and the cosmos. He sought the wisdom of the Egyptian initiates and spent twenty-two years with them. Egypt was conquered by Babylon, and in this way Pythagoras became familiar with the religions of other peoples— the Chaldeans, Persians and the Jews. He conceived the idea that all religions contain the same basic truths. After twelve years in Babylon, he returned to Greece where he restored faith in the oracle at Delphi. He stayed there for a year and then went to southern Italy where he founded a sort of university, a mystery school.

Novices were carefully selected and had to undergo trials and tests before they were admitted. He taught religion, the sciences, philosophy, psychology, but among other things he also taught the necessity of the human being's trying to improve his own nature. He said that the meaning of the universe is not to be found in what we perceive, but in what the human being produces from his own inner self. He explained that the eternal laws of existence are to be found within the human soul.

Pythagoras founded an order which was eventually attacked and dispersed by enemies, but it lasted for over two hundred and fifty years. There is much more to be said about Pythagoras and the Pythagoreans, but that would be a study for Class Ten.

PERICLES (ca. 494-429 BC)

Pericles was the most famous Athenian statesman. It is said that his manners were marked by both gravity and dignity. His integrity in financial matters was irreproachable. He was an eloquent speaker. He was trained as a soldier, but he was also a learned man. He was a pupil of Anaxagoras, one of the first of the "thinking philosophers."

Pericles characterizes the Greek attitude in his famous funeral oration, anticipating the Aristotelian approach. He says, "The barbarian goes into action because he is told to do so. We Greeks observe, think, and then act."

Pericles believed that freedom was to be found in a state where the citizens were ready to obey the laws made by themselves. He arranged a sort of parliament by having representatives chosen to it by lot. In this way, any man, rich or poor, might serve. In order that no hardship should ensue for a poor man who served, a small daily payment was made. This parliament or council managed the finances of the city, arranged public works and made the laws. With the idea that the laws made in Athens would be good for other people, Pericles waged wars of aggression against neighboring states and founded more distant colonies.

Among his many achievements, he arranged for the needy to be supported by public funds. He persuaded rich citizens to give freely in order to build a theater and buildings worthy of the city. He organized a fleet for the defense of Athens. Under his leadership, Athens became not only a beautiful city in the physical sense, but it also became the intellectual queen of the Greek states.

THUCYDIDES (471-400 BC)

As an historical figure, Thucydides is one of the most important. Before his time there were no real written records of history, and he can be considered as the first historian. He was one of the few survivors of the plague which ravaged Athens in 430 BC. For some reason which is not clear, he was exiled, but this gave him an opportunity to observe the Peloponnesian War from a distance. He was a collector of facts. He was discriminating in retelling and wrote in a condensed, concise form. He traces the developments of events, the motives of people, and the relevant relationships. He writes impartially. Thus, Thucydides presents an excellent example of the "modern" human being whose thoughts are logical and whose work is objective.

ARISTIDES (? -ca. 468 BC)

Aristides was a statesman and a general, surnamed "the Just." At the battle of Marathon he persuaded the other generals to relinquish their commands in favor of Miltiades; to this is ascribed the great victory. Through the jealousy of a rival, he was banished, but left Athens with prayers for its welfare. He returned three years later to take part in the battle of Salamis. In the battle of Plataea, he was the victorious commander. Through his influence, a law was passed in Athens giving all citizens the right to be elected magistrates. It was also due to his powers of persuasion that Athens became the center of resistance to the Persians. To meet the costs of the wars, he induced the Greeks to impose a tax, and he himself was then entrusted with the administration of it. For his honesty and integrity he became known as Aristides the Just. He died a poor man.

ALCIBIADES (450-404 BC)

It may be thought that this is not a very worthy character to describe to children, and there is justification in this. However, light and shadow go together, and we are portraying historical figures who are outstanding individualities, hence we may include Alcibiades. This was a person of great physical beauty, combined with dissoluteness of manners, determination of will, and great abilities. Socrates tried to reform him, but in vain. He was something of an irreverent buccaneer. He was an Athenian who led various military expeditions. He was accused of profaning and divulging the mysteries. He joined the Spartans, and betrayed the Athenian plans to them. He was denounced in Athens, cursed by the priests, and banished. He wandered further afield to Sparta, but engaged in intrigue to return to Athens. Here a revolution broke out. He was recalled and made commander of the fleet. Unfortunately for him, he lost the battle, was again banished, and went to Persia where he was assassinated.

SOCRATES (ca. 469-399 BC)

Among the great individualists of Greece, Socrates occupies a very important place. He had learned to be a sculptor, had studied geometry, astronomy, philosophy and had served in the army, but as far as worldly possessions were concerned, he was a poor man. He was small, with an ugly face. He was both witty and serious. In our study of Socrates there are three things of importance:

- His actual teaching
- His method
- His attitude toward life

With regard to his teaching, he believed in a divinely inspired world of which the physical was a manifestation. He believed that the gods made known their existence by their operations. He believed that reason alone could attain the truth, and he did not wish to be initiated because that would mean a seal of silence. Through his reasoning, however, he acquired the same knowledge as was taught in the mystery centers, and this he proclaimed. It was this that brought him into conflict with officialdom and led to his death sentence because—it was alleged—he had betrayed the mysteries.

He spoke of an internal voice, what we should now call conscience, but to the Greeks this was something new. Up to then, "conscience" had been experienced as something outside the human being, as was portrayed by the Furies in the drama. He believed in an inner development of the soul, such as conquering physical desires and governing the temper. His method was to teach his pupils to observe, analyse and think. Then he would cross-examine them: What is justice? What is piety? What is temperance? He wanted to lead men's minds to the eternal truths by philosophical thought. It was a sort of initiation process, but one whereby the pupil had to school his own thinking. His attitude to life was that he had a duty to perform. One might call him a reformer. The charge against him of corrupting youth is only valid if we can consider any break from tradition a corruption. In a sense, he was proclaiming the new age of reasoning.

He had some very famous pupils, but he was willing to talk to anyone, anywhere. He also succeeded in making many enemies. He considered it his duty to examine men of all degrees as to their knowledge to convince them of their ignorance that they might therefore become wise. It is not given to all men to be gracious when their ignorance is exposed, hence his unpopularity in certain quarters.

ARISTOTLE (384-322 BC)
In Aristotle, Greek philosophy achieves its peak. What had begun some three hundred years earlier as the faint gropings towards intellectual thinking is now consolidated. The power of thought has come into its own. Aristotle spent twenty years studying with the great philosopher Plato, but did not agree with his ideas, and founded his own school, the Lyceum in Athens. Like Socrates, Aristotle looked at the world in a different way from that of his predecessors, and taught his pupils to do so. He advised his students to observe, collect facts, and then come to a conclusion. This is what we call logic—following a line of ideas where one thought depends on the previous one. An example of Aristotelian logic is:

All men must die. I am a man, therefore, I must die.

His studies were universal, and he wrote down his ideas. Among the things he wrote about were space, time, the heavens, matter, nature, art, mathematics, politics, ethics, economics. He was a great biologist and made the first classification of animals. He concerned himself a great deal with the relationship between the human being and the rest of the world. For four years he was tutor to the son of Philip of Macedonia, the boy who later became known as Alexander the Great. However, the outstanding achievement of Aristotle is the demonstration of the new faculty at work in man. Three hundred years earlier men still had some perception of another world. Now this faculty had been displaced by thought. The world could be understood by the thinking process. A statement or observation was true because it could be proved by the thinking process of logic. This is a discipline in thinking processes which has lasted two thousand years.

ARCHIMEDES (ca. 287-212 BC)

In connection with the thinking processes of the mind and the direction towards the physical world, one can speak of Archimedes, one of the first scientists. Archimedes interested himself in mechanics, hydrostatics, the mathematical measurements of spheres and cylinders. He invented the compound pulley and an apparatus for raising water—the screw of Archimedes. There is also the famous discovery he made while sitting in his bath: a body immersed in a fluid loses as much in weight as the weight of an equal volume of fluid. He made a model to show how the planets revolve, and legend has it that he invented a series of levers and pulleys which were used to upset the Roman ships when they besieged his native Syracuse.

ALEXANDER THE GREAT (356-323 BC)

The other great figure who merits attention is Alexander the Great. If the teacher has the time, interest and inclination to deal with Alexander's conquests, he or she is, of course, quite at liberty to do so. In our context, however, the matter can be handled briefly so long as the important things are made clear.

According to the legend, there were, on the day of Alexander's birth, wonderful signs in the heavens, and these meant that an extraordinary child was to be born. As a youth, he had the advantage of having Aristotle as his teacher, and he undoubtedly became immersed in Aristotelian wisdom. He was educated in all branches of Hellenic culture. At the same time he was an athlete; he was courageous, daring and a born leader.

At the time of his birth, Macedonia had become the dominant state of Greece under the guidance of his father, Philip. When Philip was murdered, the young Alexander became king, at the age of twenty, and soon ruled all Greece. He became not only master of all Greece, but conquered Asia Minor, Egypt and the Persian Empire as far as the borders of India. Yet his conquests were not purely military achievements. The underlying motive was to spread Greek culture and to do it in such a way that it was not seen as an imposition, but as a fulfillment.

When the Persian emperor was murdered, Alexander took the attitude that he was heir to the Persian throne, and he took care of the royal family. On his return from India he married a Persian princess. Alexander himself sought knowledge and wisdom from the wise men of the East. He recognized common factors in all cultures and religions, and wanted to synthesize these. He recognized that the divine power which had been made manifest through the old gods was now working in the mind of man—in his conscience, in his thinking. Because of his understanding for the older cultures, he was accepted by their peoples as a spiritual leader. Wherever he went, he founded academies of learning. The most famous center and the one which lasted the longest was Alexandria in Egypt. Here, all streams of culture were brought together, Egypto-Chaldean, Babylonian, Greek and Hebrew.

After ten years in the field, which took him to the borders of India, he returned to Babylon where he developed a fever and died. He was thirty-three. Alexander had felt that he had a divine mission to unite Europe and Asia, and to make Greek culture world culture.

Rome

Rome shows us a vastly different picture, and the method of presentation can be somewhat different. At the age of twelve, the child's intellectual capacity is growing and he or she is beginning to be able to grasp abstract concepts. It is therefore possible and educationally correct to give more details and explanations. Twelve is also the age of puberty, when children become much more aware of their physical bodies and of the material world around them. They discover that they are individuals among other individuals, and an adjustment of relationships is necessary. The story of Rome, with its outstanding interest in materialistic things and human rights, parallels the development of the child of twelve, and it is therefore educationally beneficial.

We mentioned earlier the main trends of the Graeco-Roman epoch. These were: interest in the physical world, development of individuality, intellectual thinking. The manifestations were different in the different civilizations. In Greece, we see them in philosophical thought, in art, and in the social order of the city-states. In Rome, the outlines become much sharper.

Rome appears as the physical conquerer of the world, with acquisition of wealth, riches, and worldly power as aims. The very land on which it grew was conquered territory. Physical courage was praised; the physical conquerer was honored.

The feeling of individuality manifests itself in the endless struggles to find an acceptable social system and in the establishment of law. The citizen had his rights, and his vote was based on his own views. As an individual, he felt his own personality, but realized that there were also others with their rights. In case of a dispute, the earlier peoples had referred it to the deity, or to the divinely inspired ruler, but the Roman appointed a man, a judge, a third party, whose decision was binding , and who followed a set code.

The development of individuality also shows in the dissolution of ties of blood relationship. In early times in Rome, property belonged to the head of the household, but later, the son could be an owner in his own right. Formerly, a son would have had to pay his father's debts, but this obligation was eventually cancelled. Symptomatic also was the making of wills. This was a Roman invention. Romans felt the necessity of expressing their will in the world even after death.

Although a select few ruled at first, in the course of time it became possible for anyone, irrespective of race or color, to become a magistrate or an official. These were elective posts. Even the emperors were not always of Roman birth. Trajan was a Spaniard, Diocletian, a Dalmatian peasant. Eventually, all free persons in the empire became Roman citizens, which meant that they could vote in the assembly—if they could get there.

The growing powers of thinking do not show themselves in their application to philosophy, but in practical matters. The

Romans understood town planning, building of fortifications, surveying, mining, engineering. They provided their buildings with a form of central heating, had good water supplies and sanitation. They had oil lamps and water clocks. Boys were educated in grammar, spelling and the law. A sense of duty was inculcated. Whereas the Greek boys had learned Homer, the Roman learned the law—by heart. It is significant that the Romans adopted the Latin language—a cold, logical, unemotional medium. Let us also note that the educated person of those times was not the philosopher of the Greeks, nor the learned doctor of the future middle ages, but the orator-lawyer.

Teachers may like to give further information on everyday life in Rome, and support their teaching with drawings or paintings, but these things are easily obtainable from textbooks. Children could even read some suitable books for themselves. Here, we wish to pursue our own theme.

From a handful of adventurers, and from small beginnings, Rome spread out north, south, east and west, and became a mighty empire, incorporating many different peoples and lands. As its power grew, it took the place of Greece as the center of the known world. All roads led to Rome. The Roman conquered the physical world and established the law. There was no longer any real spiritual direction. We spoke of the Greek as living in a twilight world where the gods still wielded some influence. The Roman descended to the earth and created a social life based solely on arrangements made between human beings.

The mystery centers and the oracles of the Greeks became the temples and the augurs of the Romans. There was a very apparent de-spiritualization. Religion and worship became almost a façade. It is true that some Romans considered themselves pious and religious. We might say the same of many modern Christians. Cicero wrote, "We Romans owe our supremacy over all other peoples to our piety and religious observances, and to our wisdom in believing that the spirit of the gods rules and directs everything." Perhaps he believed it. Perhaps the Romans, like many others, found that many happenings in the world are inexplicable in material terms, and the mind therefore turns easily to thoughts of the supernatural. The ancient peoples had perceived spiritually. The Romans did not have the vision, but there remained no doubt a tradition, and with the idea that "there might be something in it," they acknowledged the gods. In the main, they adopted the Greek deities, changed their names, and looked upon them as functional agents. Thus there were different gods for different functions or localities. There were gods of the weather, of growth, of groves, rivers, lakes, as well as a god of war and a goddess of love. Temples were erected. Offerings or sacrifices were made in the belief that the gods would then look favorably on the suppliants. It was usually some personal or self-ish thing that was desired, perhaps a petition, a personal favor, or the curing of an illness. The whole affair had the air of striking a bargain.

There were no religious ceremonies for the public. The priests were required to say the formulae and to make supplica-tions for such public enterprises as going to war. It was felt that the gods had a right to sacrifices and worship, but that they should reciprocate by helping the state and the citizens. The Augurs were another type of functionary. They were almost the official prophets. They noted the flight of birds, or read signs from the entrails of some animal which had been sacrificed. The sacrifices took place in the open air on special altars outside the temples. Every home had a domestic shrine to reverence the god-dess of fire, Vesta, and there would be a little daily ceremony with gifts. She was the protecting spirit of the house and had to be placated.

In the course of time, Rome absorbed many other peoples and religions. On the principle of making sure that no deity should be offended, the Romans built the Pantheon and dedicat-ed it to all the gods. Tiberius and Hadrian even toyed with the idea of including Christ.

There was, however, a more subtle reason for bringing the images of the gods of the different peoples to Rome. The god rep-resented a sort of folk spirit, and when his image was removed, the people became demoralized, thus making domination by the conquerer easier.

Otherwise in religious matters, the Romans were tolerant. As long as the subjugated peoples observed the Roman festivals and acknowledged the god-emperor, they could worship other gods privately. The Jews and the Christians could not, of course, rec-oncile themselves to this, hence the persecutions.

Rome seems very much nearer to us than Greece, especially in England, and the approach is therefore easier. We mentioned earlier some of the connections between Rome and England. This information can now well be extended.

Many of our cities are of Roman origin. Londinium has become London; Dubris, Dover; Lindum, Lincoln; Eboracum, York; Isca Dumnoniorum, Exeter; Deva Castra, Chester (the fort on the River Dee). The endings *-chester* or *-cester* as in Leicester, Worcester, Winchester, Silchester, Colchester, signify a Roman fort in the locality. Some Roman settlements have, in the meantime, acquired other names: Aqua Sulis, Bath; Verulamium, St. Albans.

Roman roads crisscross the country. There is the Watling Street from Dover via London to Chester; the Fosse Way from Exeter via Bath and Leicester to Lincoln; Ermin Street from London via Lincoln and York to Corbridge. Interesting too, is the Sarn Helen in Wales, the road connecting the castles of the British princess who became the wife of a Roman emperor.

In various parts of the country are the remains of Roman villas, amphitheatres, forums, forts, etc., among which might be mentioned and described: the baths at Bath, the fort at Richborough, Hadrian's Wall, the theatre at St. Albans, the lighthouse at Dover. The Romans were the first to cultivate systematically the land of England. They introduced the cabbage, onion, apple and the rose. The South Downs were a great corn-growing area. Britain was known as the "Granary of the North."

The Romans were our first miners. They extracted tin, coal, lead, copper, gold. They have bequeathed to us the names of measurements. Our [British] penny (the former d.) was the Roman *denarius*. Our mile is from the Roman *mille passus* (thousand paces). Our pound is from the Latin *pondus*, meaning weight. Most of the names of the months are Roman in origin. Looking a little further into Europe, we find the Roman legacy also in the languages spoken, for instance, French, Spanish, Italian, Romanian. These are matters which children of twelve will find extraordinarily interesting.

We can now turn to the land itself where the Roman civilization began. Italy is the modern name of the country about which we are talking. Two thousand years ago it had no such name. Before Rome was founded, it was inhabited by various peoples such as the Etruscans, Sabines, Latins and Greek colonists. It is a long peninsula stretching southward from the Alps into the warm waters of the Mediterranean. It has the sea on three sides, and the mountains in the north form a considerable barrier to the rest of Europe. It has a backbone of mountains, narrow but fertile plains, few rivers or ports. Unlike Greece, it has a straight coast-line and very few offshore islands. It is a sunny land and produces crops such as vines, olives, figs, mulberries, cherries, pomegranates, maize, barley, oats and wheat. On the hills are forests of oak and chestnut. It has two volcanoes.

As we have seen in other instances where a new impulse is to develop, there is first a mixing of peoples. We shall see from the legends and the historical facts that the first inhabitants of Rome were very doubtful characters. They established themselves and conquered their immediate neighbors, in those days, the Latins, Sabines and Etruscans, even adopting the Latin language. As they expanded, more peoples were incorporated, and the blood became very mixed. Such people as came together to found and develop Roman civilization had, of necessity, to find the law to regulate relationships. The iron military discipline arose from the same background. Thus we can understand the essentially new developments which centered around the ideas of citizenship. These were: the rights of the human being as a citizen and the political structure of the state. The great achievement of the Romans was to establish a political state with a universal code of laws.

In dealing with Greece, we suggested four themes: the mythology, political development, historical events and biographies. The actual story of Rome is, of course, available in history books. It is therefore intended to give only an outline here, together with such other contributions as are befitting, to our particular object. For the most part, explanations are unnecessary. The unfolding of events and the descriptions which the teacher gives to the children will convey what we wish them to understand.

As far as Rome is concerned, there is very little in the way of mythology, but legends and actual happenings take its place. The other themes can be used. One of the most significant legends is the one concerned with the founding of Rome.

When the Greeks sacked Troy, one of the Trojan princes, Aeneas, escaped and sailed away to what we now call Italy. He sailed up one of the rivers. His son, Ascanius, founded a settlement there which was given the name of Alba Longa. Many years later, one of the kings of Alba Longa had two sons who quarrelled over the succession. One of them, Numitor by name, should have become king, but he was ousted by his brother,

Amulius. Numitor's daughter was sent to serve in the temple. Here she was visited by the god Mars, and subsequently bore twin boys, Romulus and Remus. When this became known to the usurper, he ordered the boys to be thrown into the river. However, they did not drown, but were cast ashore and found by a she-wolf who suckled them. Later, a shepherd found them and brought them up. When they were grown men, they happened to be brought before Numitor, who recognized them as his grandsons. Eventually, Amulius was killed and the throne was restored to its rightful owner.

With some followers, the two brothers now left Alba Longa to found their own city, but they could not agree on a site. They therefore looked for omens. Remus observed six vultures, which were considered sacred birds; but Romulus saw twelve. Opinion was on his side, so Romulus drew a furrow where the walls of the city should be built; where the gates were to stand, the plow was lifted over the space. He decreed that the "city" should be entered only by the "gates" and set a guard to see that his orders were carried out. In defiance, Remus jumped the "wall" and was slain. The city was built. Romulus became the first king and gave the city his name. He invited all fugitives to join him. There was a shortage of women, so the neighboring tribe of Sabines was robbed of maidens. Legend says that when Romulus died, his father, Mars, carried him up to heaven in a cloud. The date of the founding of Rome is usually considered to be 753 BC.

The whole of this story, fact or fiction, is significant. The connection with Troy shows that the new culture is the sequel to the previous one. Mars, the god of war, is the father of the twins. The boys are cast out, homeless, that is, they have a special destiny in being unrestricted. They are suckled by a wolf, a picture of the dark forces of materialism. We are reminded of the Fenris Wolf of northern mythology who swallows the sun. Vultures, birds of prey, provide the omens. When Romulus marks the positions of the walls, it is perhaps symbolic of the limited earthly consciousness. Remus is still a little other-worldly and finds it difficult to accept. He is killed by his brother; that is to say that from now on, consciousness is to be of physical things. Thus, the story of Rome opens with fratricide—a pointer, too, to the ending of the blood relationships.

Romulus now invites fugitives to join him. So there stream towards the new city hosts of foreign elements of the worst sort:

adventurers, robbers, brigands, murderers, people with no blood ties or traditions—just the type of persons who would have to be governed by some system of law. Even marriage and the production of future citizens was only accomplished by force. The mixed elements must have settled down fairly rapidly, and since food is of prime concern, the early Romans turned to farming with a readiness to fight for their city collectively if need arose.

We can see then that in these legends there is a tremendous content. They are a prologue to the achievement of the Roman civilization which was to establish the law as between person and person.

THE POLITICAL DEVELOPMENTS

The first rulers were kings and they ruled by popular will. They were not hereditary, and again we must note the significance of the individual, "the man for the job," in modern parlance. One was a Sabine, one a Greek noble, one a former slave, and several were Etruscans. When Tarquinius Superbus seized the throne and became a tyrant, he was deposed. The monarchy was abolished.

The reign of the seven kings was, as it were, an echo of earlier times. It was no longer appropriate in evolution that one person should rule and the rest follow. There has to be guidance in the form of government, but the citizen now creates that government. The burning of the Sibylline books also shows the changing times.

The original inhabitants of Rome were known as the Patricians, and at first the political power was in their hands. They represent the old family-blood relationship which was to be superseded in favor of the individual. They had an assembly known as the *Comitia Curiata*, which made the laws. From the members and by the members of this assembly was elected the Senate (Council of Elders) to advise the king.

There were two other classes, the *Clients* and the *Plebeians*. The Clients were particular friends of the Patricians, who had been invited by them, sponsored by them, and who were dependent on them. The Plebeians were the rest of the people. The division was into a ruling class and a ruled, but not in any sense like the aristocracy and the working class of England, since both Patricians and Plebeians might be of any rank or station, educated or otherwise. It was purely a matter of being native or foreign, though the distinction is somewhat blurred.

Servius Tullius, the third king, made the first change by dividing the whole populace into five classes based on wealth, and this determined taxation and voting rights. There was also an arrangement whereby the votes of older citizens carried more weight than those of the younger. The result of this reform was that the Plebeians had equal power with the Patricians on the basis of wealth. The representatives of these voters formed a national assembly known as the *Comitia Centuriata*. The highest functions of the Comitia Curiata were transferred to this body, but the Senate had still to ratify their decisions.

When the kings were abolished in 509 BC, the republic was established. The leadership of the state was put into the hands of two elected magistrates, and we should note both the appellation and the number. The magistrate was a civil officer administering the law. Later, the heads of state were known as *consuls*, which means advisers. Only Patricians were eligible, and they served for one year. If we used a modern term for magistrate or consul in this sense, the nearest we could get would probably be "president." The fact that there were two shows a desire for balance. Each had the right of veto. We see that the divinely inspired guidance of earlier times under a priest-king has given way to human leadership which must be watched and limited. At the same time, the functions of state and religion were separated. There were now "presidents" and priests. In times of stress or emergency, one person could be elected to take overall direction. He was known as the *Dictator*. Dictatorship meant military rule and suspension of constitutional guarantees, the sole right of making peace or war, and the use of the treasury funds.

For the next two hundred years, the Plebeians struggled with the Patricians to establish their rights. The Plebeians elected two magistrates, called *tribunes*, to represent them, then five, later ten. These officials had a right of veto to prevent injustice to a citizen.

One of the bones of contention was concerning public land, that is, land taken from neighboring tribes. Since, at first, Rome was a farming community, land was very valuable and should have been shared. The Patricians, however, as the dominant party, acquired most of the newly conquered territory to the exclusion of the Plebeians. Another cause of dissatisfaction was that in the course of time only Plebeians were called upon to serve in the army. They had to provide their own equipment, and while on service, their fields were neglected.

Yet a greater source of unrest was that only Patricians could be judges and originally they had somewhat arbitrary powers. This fact induced the Plebeians to demand written laws. It was agreed that this should be done, and ten men, the *Decemvirate*, were appointed, with unlimited powers to carry out the task. In 451 BC, they produced ten tables of laws, and in the next year a further two, making up the famous Laws of the Twelve Tables. Unfortunately, the Decemvirate refused to resign their office at the appointed time and were only removed by an insurrection.

Thus the Plebeians gained more power and now demanded an assembly which was fully representative. This became known as the *Comitia Tributa*, and it became the effective law-making body. Its resolutions had to be confirmed by the other two comitia and by the senate, but in the course of time this became a matter of form. The senate retained certain functions such as administering the public treasury, appointing ambassadors and provincial governors and signing treaties. Later, the Comitia Centuriata and the Comitia Tributa became fused.

In 445 BC, the Plebeians achieved the *connubium,* i.e., the right of intermarriage with Patricians without loss of rank to the offspring of the marriage. In time, the Plebeians also achieved the right to become candidates for the highest offices, and in 366 BC, all exclusive privileges of the Patricians ended. One might think that the struggle of the common people for their rights was over, but now it took a new form, one with which we are all too familiar today. A new nobility of officials and bureaucrats developed. The wealthy of both classes now took the privileges. They took over management of the provinces and the positions of state; they expropriated private property and generally served their own interests. There was, of course, opposition, instanced by the story of the Gracchi (to follow).

In the meantime, Rome was expanding and citizenship was extended. In 89 BC, all the free inhabitants of Italy became citizens of the city of Rome, which meant that they could vote in the assembly—if they could get there. (In AD 212, every free man in the Roman Empire became a Roman citizen.) In 81 BC, the consul Sulla tried to re-establish the original constitution of rule by the few, but failed.

In 60 BC, the so-called *Triumvirate* was formed. This consisted of three men, Julius Caesar, Pompey and Crassus. These three took the government into their own hands, but it soon became clear that there was rivalry between Caesar and Pompey. Crassus was a less forceful character. Pompey believed in a more aristocratic form of government, while Caesar leaned towards democracy. At least he gave the appearance of so doing and gained popular support. Pompey fled. Julius Caesar was made dictator. With that act one could almost say that the Roman experiment came to an end. From that time onwards, although the law was established, dictators and emperors were to rule. It was a return to the type of despotic rule of earlier civilizations, but by men without spiritual guidance; or perhaps when one studies the records of later emperors one might conclude that there was some spiritual guidance, but it was demonic.

The rot did not set in at once. Julius Caesar instituted many reforms and apparently ruled well. Rightly or wrongly, he was accused of usurping too much power and was murdered. A second Triumvirate was formed consisting of Octavianus (Julius Caesar's nephew and adopted son), Lepidus and Mark Antony. As with the first Triumvirate, rivalry broke out between the two most powerful characters, and Antony fled to Egypt. Octavianus followed and captured Egypt, adding it to the Roman domain. Octavianus Caesar was now all-powerful. He was given the title *Augustus*, and became the first emperor of Rome. The Republic was at an end.

As a ruler and an administrator, Augustus was efficient and benevolent. He made many reforms. He arranged for a general assembly to be held once a year in the provincial capitals. He organized a universal system of justice, taking local customs into account. Punishment was meted out according to rank and intelligence. There was also punishment for criminal intention. In the courts, the accusers had to face the accused and give verbal evidence. Poor people could have free legal aid. With Augustus began the *Pax Romana*, peace in the Roman Empire, which lasted for two hundred years. With the establishment of peace and safe communications, trade flourished. A great flow of goods came into the capital. From Gaul in the north came wool and agricultural products. From Spain came fruit and metals; from the east, spices. In Syria grew the famous cedar trees, while North Africa was an immense corn-growing area. People could travel safely from one end of the Empire to the other and settle anywhere.

Yet the Pax Romana had its shadow side. It was a peace imposed by the sword. The peoples of the Empire were very mixed, but Rome did not interfere in language, customs, tradition, or religion except when they came into conflict with Roman law. Then the Romans were ruthless. When it was thought that the priests of the Gauls, the Druids, might still be influential, they were utterly destroyed.

Augustus adhered to most of the republican forms of government. The senate became a council of state; magistrates were elected, but gradually Augustus acquired all the high offices. He became the ruler, consul, the people's representative, chief priest, and was finally pronounced divine—*dominus et deus*. It is the climax of the drama. No longer do the gods speak. A man is deified. Caesar is elevated to a god. He denies in the senate the immortality of the soul. Rome is a vast worldly empire and there is no world beyond. Remember the wolf. Rome has reached its peak, and Roman civilization its nadir. During the reign of Augustus, an event took place in an outlying part of the Empire which was to prove of far greater importance in world history:

> And it came to pass in those days, that there went out a decree from Caesar Augustus, that all the world should be taxed. And all went to be taxed, everyone into his own city. And Joseph also went up from Galilee, out of the city of Nazareth, into Judea, unto the city of David, which is called Bethlehem; because he was of the house and lineage of David, to be taxed with Mary, his espoused wife, being great with child. And so it was, that, while they were there, the days were accomplished that she should be delivered. And she brought forth her first born son, and wrapped him in swaddling clothes, and laid him in a manger; because there was no room for them in the inn.

Interestingly enough, in the period immediately before the birth of Christ, there were many references to the coming of a world ruler. Whether these refer to the one whose kingdom is of this world, or to the one whose kingdom is not of this world, is a matter of interpretation. The Roman historian Suetonius wrote:

> In ancient days part of the city wall of Velitrae had been struck by lightning and the soothsayers prophesied that a native Velitraean would one day rule the world [Caesar Augustus was born in Velitrae]. According to Julius

Marathus, a public portent warned the Roman people some months before Augustus' birth that Nature was making ready to provide them with a king.

The Empire lasted for another four hundred years, but the story became one of decline, degradation and disintegration. Many Romans had grown rich, lazy and depraved. Slaves were so plentiful that they did all the work, and the poorer citizens were unemployed. The value of money went down. There was inflation. The collection of taxes was inefficient. There was graft and bribery among the officials. The legions were manned by provincials. The assemblies ceased to function. Corn was provided free, and the people had to be distracted by entertainments. They were given "bread and circuses." The circuses were horrible spectacles, and included chariot racing, gladiatorial shows, throwing Christians to the lions, fighting wild beasts. The army made emperors or disposed of them.

To complete the historical outline, a few of the more outstanding events could be described: the destruction of Jerusalem, 70 AD; the conquest of Britain, 77 AD; the division of the Empire into east and west; the recognition of Christianity under Constantine; the Visigoth invasion under Alaric; the final collapse of the Western Empire in 476 AD; the codification of laws and the closing of the schools of philosophy in Athens by Justinian, 529 AD. It is worth pointing out that a code of laws is something static and petrified. This is a theme to be re-introduced in the Upper School when discussing the social order.

THE DEVELOPMENT OF CHRISTIANITY

Christ's teaching of love, forgiveness and the Kingdom of Heaven was something for which the Romans had little understanding, but through the disciples his message was spread far afield. The first sympathizers were in the Greek world—the majority of Paul's letters were to the Greek communities. Many people in Syria, Asia Minor and Greece became *Christiani*, the Roman term. In the year 60 AD, St. Paul was proclaiming the gospel in Rome itself. The Christians felt that they could not keep the Roman festivals, nor could they worship the emperor as god. They were therefore attacked, murdered, crucified, and thrown to the lions to provide entertainment for the bloodthirsty masses.

In spite of this, their numbers grew. People, including soldiers, wondered how they could remain steadfast in the face of such persecution. Admiration and understanding brought converts. Learned men became interested and were able to explain the Christian way to others. For some time the Christians in Rome were driven to living in the catacombs, burial places for the dead, but still their numbers grew.

In the year 305 AD, the reigning emperor died and the soldiers of the west proclaimed Constantine, who was then at York, his successor. The peoples of the eastern half of the empire did not agree, and a struggle arose, eventually decided by war. Before a decisive battle, Constantine prayed to his father's god "the unconquered sun," and had a vision of the cross and heard the words: "Conquer with this." He put a cross on his standard, went into battle, and was victorious. Later, in the year 313 AD, he proclaimed that there should be freedom of religion in all the empire. Constantine realized that Rome was no longer the best-situated city to be capital. Accordingly, he chose another place, the ancient city of Byzantium—modern Istanbul. He renamed it Constantinople, and rebuilt it in magnificent style. The new city was to be Christian and Latin. It remained Christian, but older influences were strong, and the Greek language was retained. Constantine was baptized a Christian on his death-bed in 337 AD.

This is about as far as one can go in Class Six with these themes. It could be indicated, however, that as Christianity became recognized and was made into the state religion, so it became Romanized. The church adopted the structure of the Roman state and its way of thinking. The original impulse and understanding were destroyed. Truth was no longer by revelation, but attainable through discussion and committees. This had a far-reaching effect which is suitable for study later on.

CONQUESTS AND COLLAPSE
We have spoken of the conquest of the physical world. The Romans achieved this in its literal sense. At this stage in school life there is neither time nor necessity to enter into detail, but an outline is essential. The study can be supported by drawing maps. The Romans also made conquests in another sense. They romanized Christianity and their code of laws became the pat-

tern for the legal system of many European states. The beginnings of Rome are legendary. During the reign of the kings, from 753 to 509 BC, the story is one of struggles with the immediate neighbors, who are conquered, subjugated and assimilated. In 491 BC, there was war with the Volsci, from which comes the story of Coriolanus. There was war with the Veii in 477 BC.

The Romans did not have it all their own way. In 390 B.C., the Gauls captured Rome and sacked it, but the citizens were resilient. They returned and recaptured the city, continued to expand their territorial conquests and were masters of all Italy by the year 275 BC.

There were three wars with Carthage, a Phoenician settlement in North Africa. These were known as the Punic wars. (Punic comes from *Poeni* = Phoenician.) They took place between the years 264 and 146 BC during which time the Romans found it necessary to build a fleet. They were finally victorious, and Carthage was utterly destroyed. *"Carthago delendum est,"* are the famous words given to Scipio, the army commander. It was during the second of these wars that the Carthaginian general Hannibal made his famous march across Spain and France, crossing the Alps in winter with his elephants and penetrating into Italy. This is a story which always fires the imagination.

The Punic wars were actually an echo of the Greek-Trojan struggle. It was a fight between east and west, with the Phoenicians representing the old patriarchal style of life and the Romans the individualistic. About the year 200 BC, there was a lull in the Punic wars and the Romans turned eastwards. Greece became a vassal state and was known as the province of Achaia in 146 BC. This brought the Romans into much closer contact with Greek thought and art, much of which they adopted. Thus, although Rome conquered Greece physically, in another sense, Greece conquered Rome. Expansion continued into Asia Minor. Syria was conquered in 64, Judea in 63 BC.

In the west, the present region of Provence in the south of France became Roman in 125 BC. (For student travellers this is an area rich in Roman remains: triumphal arches, amphitheaters, temples, aqueducts, the cities of Nimes and Arles.) With the advent of Julius Caesar as consul in 59 BC, Gaul was conquered and expeditions were made to England. Under Augustus, the first emperor, Roman rule extended from the Atlantic to the Euphrates, from the Rhine and Danube to the deserts of Africa.

Albion (England) was added in 77 AD, and under Trajan, who ruled from 98 to 117, further provinces were acquired north of the Danube. Territorial expansion had reached its greatest extent. Roman influence spread itself over the greater part of the known world. The empire formed a cohesive territory in which the growth of Christianity could take place.

After Augustus, there was a steady decline. Internally, the state became rotten and was no longer equal to repelling attacks from outside. Some emperors ruled as tyrants, some were mad, a few were wise. Hadrian was one of the good rulers. He visited all parts of the empire personally to check the administration. It was in his reign, 117 to 138, that the great wall was built across the north of England. It was also in his reign that the final dispersion of the Jews took place after a revolt (132-135 AD).

Marcus Aurelius is remembered as a philosopher as well as an emperor. He lived a simple life with high ideals, but made the mistake of thinking that other men were moved by high motives. His wise government could not stop disturbances created by others, and during his reign there was continual strife on the eastern frontiers. Soldiers returning from the east also brought the plague with them. This spread, devastating Rome and all Italy.

The Empire had become unwieldy and difficult to administer. Therefore, in 292, Diocletian, with three associate rulers, divided it into four parts. Constantine united it again in 323, and moved the capital to Byzantium. It was divided again in 395 into east and west, and never again united.

Along the Rhine and Danube frontiers lived the tribes of restless, warlike, energetic and adventurous Teutons (*Germanii*). The Roman historian Tacitus says that they had the secret of political liberty, individual initiative, renovating power, and large families. The most troublesome of the Teutons were the Goths. Those who lived around the Black Sea were known as the Ostrogoths, and those further west were the Visigoths.

Suddenly, a movement of people began from the direction of Central Asia. A wild Mongolian people came into Europe, sweeping everything before them. They were the Huns, led by Attila. The Visigoths were the first to be attacked, but they made an arrangement with the emperor of Constaninople to enter Roman territory. However, they soon decided to annex part of this for themselves and under their leader, Alaric, they crossed into Greece, plundering the cities on the way. They made their way into Italy, captured and plundered Rome, then made their way into France and Spain. In the meantime, another wild race, the Vandals, had wandered from the shores of the Baltic through Spain to North Africa. Crossing the sea, they also sacked Rome before retreating to the Carthage area. To meet these attacks, the Roman legions were called in from the provinces. As they left Britain, that country was open to attacks by the pirate Anglo-Saxons. When they left the Rhine, Teutonic tribes crossed it—the Franks into Gaul, others into modern Belgium. Clovis was the king of the Franks, and under his rule the present country of France began to take shape. Paris was the capital.

Attila, meanwhile, ruled Europe from the Rhine to the Urals and exacted tribute from both western and eastern empires. A combined Roman and Gothic army met his forces at Châlons and defeated him. Attila recovered, crossed the Alps and marched on Rome. Outside the city walls he was met by the pope and he withdrew, agreeing to accept tribute. Attila returned to his head-quarters on the Danube, but suddenly died. The Huns scattered and were seen no more.

The last Roman emperor in the west was installed through the support of one of the German tribes, but failed to keep his bargain. The leader, Odoacer, therefore deposed him and proclaimed himself king of Italy. The year was 476 AD. The eastern empire lasted until 1204. As the political power of Rome vanished, its influence made itself felt in other ways, through the Roman Catholic church, and through its legal system which became a pattern for much of Europe. Thus, we could say that Rome made conquests in three spheres: territory, religion and law.

BIOGRAPHIES
Reference to historical personalities can be a great help in the teaching of history. In this instance, not only do biographies illustrate the developing individuality, but the people concerned are intimately bound up with the historical events. It may not be possible to include all which are here suggested in the actual history period, but there is no reason why the study should not be extended into the English lessons and over a longer period of time. In any case, the teacher must make his own choice. The following short summaries are offered as indications.

SERVIUS TULLIUS

Legend has it that Servius Tullius was the son of a slave in the palace of Tarquin, the fifth king of Rome. One day the queen saw a flame around his head, which she took as a sign from heaven, and he was henceforth brought up as a prince. He rose to a position of eminence, and Tarquin gave him his daughter in marriage. He was popular with the people and the army. He succeeded to the throne on the death of his father-in-law in 578 BC, by popular will. He organized a census and the national assemblies, built temples, beautified the city and extended its boundaries.

His reforms did not make him beloved by everyone. His daughters were married to the sons of his father-in-law, one of whom was covetous and wished to restore the old form of despotic rule. He had Servius assassinated and seized the throne for himself. This was Tarquinius Superbus (the proud), but he proved too much for the Romans, who banished him and never again had kings as rulers.

CINCINNATUS (ca. 519 BC)

This was a character to whom the Romans looked up with great respect. He was born about 519 BC, in the early days of Rome when there was much quarrelling between the patricians and the plebeians. He himself was a patrician, had been an official and a general in the army, but had retired to his country estate. An enemy suddenly attacked Rome and a Roman army was surrounded. Cincinnatus was at work in his fields when the delegation from the senate arrived to offer him the dictatorship. He accepted, organized a new force, rescued the trapped army, gained a victory, and returned to his farm—all within sixteen days. At the age of eighty he was recalled again to the dictatorship to negotiate a settlement between the upper and lower classes. In this too, he was successful.

HORATIUS

The story of how Horatius kept the bridge (507 BC) is to be found in Macaulay's *Lays of Ancient Rome*. It is an excellent piece for recitation.

CORIOLANUS

The Romans were at war with the Volsci. Caius Marcius was a soldier who was instrumental in capturing the enemy city of Corioli, and hence was accorded the title of honor, Coriolanus. He was a proud, haughty patrician, who had made himself unpopular with the plebians during the famine of 490 BC, when there had been disputes over the distribution of corn. He made no headway with the common people when it was necessary to seek their support in an election. He was so insulting that he was banished. He was incensed at this treatment, joined the enemy forces, and with them marched on Rome. He was only dissuaded from attacking by the appeals of his wife and mother, particularly the latter. His choice lay between storming Rome with his new allies, or suffering a probable death at their hands. He spared the city and was murdered by the Volsci. "O Mother, you have saved Rome, but lost a son," were the words put into his mouth by Shakespeare. It is too early to study Shakespeare's plays systematically, but the teacher may find it useful to refer to them.

THE FABII

This was a distinguished and well-known family in the early days of Rome. When an attack was made on this city by an enemy in 477 BC, all except one of the members of the family who could bear arms—306 in number—went with 4000 clients to meet the enemy. All died except the one who happened to have been left behind. His descendants became prominent figures. Among them was Fabius Maxim Cunctator, the opponent of Hannibal in the Second Punic War. He received the title *Cunctator*, which means "delayer," on account of his tactics. He kept Hannibal and his army on the move without offering battle, thus wearing them down.

TIBERIUS AND CAIUS GRACCHUS

The events described took place about the year 130 BC. The Gracchus family was a distinguished one. Tiberius had earned himself a name in the army and had been a tribune. He was concerned with the poverty of many of the citizens of Rome. He wanted the land to be redistributed, and for this purpose he revived an old law which limited the amount of land which any one person could hold, but which had not been enforced. This met with determined opposition by the landowners who tried to stop him but could not in the face of popular demand.

The actual execution of the plan proved almost impossible administratively, and was, of course, not helped by the opposition. People became disillusioned, and Tiberius lost some of his popularity. At the time of the next election, vast numbers of people were gathered in the Forum, and an actual battle took place between the supporters of the landowners and those demanding reform. In this tumult, Tiberius was slain.

The struggle over the land question continued. Ten years later, the younger brother, Caius, became tribune. As a reformer he had some success. He supported the law on the distribution of the land and succeeded in getting many of its enemies expelled from the city. He arranged that corn should be sold to the poor at a low, fixed rate. He caused new highways to be built; he introduced a new form of insurance for the soldiers. The common people were delighted, but the aristocrats embittered. The latter took into their pay a tribune-elect who made greater promises of reform. By this means Caius was outvoted and lost his tribuneship. In a new tumult, he suffered the same fate as his brother.

JULIUS CAESAR
As a pure biography, the life of Julius Caesar is probably one of the most interesting. Like Nelson, who was a frail little boy and always suffered from sea-sickness, Julius Caesar had an illness to contend with, probably epilepsy.

He was born about the year 100 BC, and belonged to the patrician class. He was rich, ambitious and self-willed. He had to flee the city for a time for not complying with an order which he considered unjust. He was captured by pirates and spent some time with them. In spite of his position, he gave orders to them and threatened them, at which they laughed. But Caesar was in earnest, and when his ransom had been paid, he hired ships to search out these pirates, who were captured and then crucified.

He had an excellent memory and an excellent mind for business. He became an eloquent speaker and, later, a fluent writer. (What Latin scholar has not read *De Bello Gallico* and had the opening words imprinted on his or her mind forever: *"Omnia*

Gallia divisa est in partes tres"?) He was popular with the people and was elected High Priest, to the annoyance of some of the senate members and nobles.

To get him out of the way for a time, he was given command of the army in Spain. Here he was victorious, and returned to Rome, where he was made consul. Together with Pompey and Crassus, he formed the Triumvirate, but it soon became clear that the combination would not hold. Caesar now demanded the governorship of Gaul for five years, and this was granted. During this time he subjugated the territories which we now call North Italy, Switzerland, France and Belgium, and made them tributaries to Rome. Twice he landed with expeditionary forces in Britain. In other parts of the empire, Pompey was having his successes. He fought many victorious battles in Africa and Asia, and cleared the seas of pirates.

Both men were capable, successful generals, but Caesar was probably the more astute, gaining the good will of the people by an apparent show of sympathy with democratic ideas. It became clear that there would be a struggle for mastery.

Caesar was returning from his conquest of Gaul with his army when he came to the Rubicon, a small river in the north of Italy which was the boundary at that time. He knew that if he crossed with his army, it would mean civil war. After he had made that fateful crossing, the two forces did not engage at once, and Pompey withdrew to Greece. Caesar, however, pursued him and was victorious at the battle of Pharsalia. Pompey fled to Egypt and was murdered. Caesar followed and eventually added Egypt to the Roman Empire.

When he returned to Rome in 46 BC, he was appointed dictator for ten years, then for life. He redistributed some of the land in favor of the poor; he improved the laws and he reformed the army and the navy. He was the most powerful man in the world. He received honor upon honor, was given entire control of the treasury and the title *imperator*, which meant that the control of the army was bestowed upon him. There was only one honor left—to name him king. (We see the cycle of development. The wheel has turned full circle, but the decline begins.)

Rumors began to spread that Caesar wished to be king. Some nobles spread the idea for their own ends, while others acted out of a sense of patriotism, thinking that Caesar might really become too powerful. The title was anathema to the citizens. A plot was hatched to kill him, and he was murdered on his way to the senate on March 15th, 44 BC.

(*"Et tu, Brute."* See Shakespeare's *Julius Caesar.*)

CALIGULA

Here is an example of a return to earlier conditions of rule, justified so long as humanity was living in a group consciousness, and the ruler was inspired. Now, this type of rule becomes tyranny, and of the worst sort, as one gets the impression that Caligula was possessed by some Satanic power.

At first, Caligula was welcomed as emperor. His first acts were an amnesty for prisoners, cancellation of banishments, prohibition of all prosecutions for treason. More freedom and independence were given to the magistrates. Then he seems to have become deranged. He ate his meals while watching people being tortured. He built a bridge over part of the sea, with soil and houses on it, so that he could boast of marching over the sea on dry land. He held a banquet on it to celebrate the achievement, and then had his guests thrown into the water. He claimed to have conquered nature.

He made huge preparations for undertakings which he never fulfilled. He wanted to murder many members of the senate. His horse had a house and servant, and was admitted to the college of priests. He wanted to make his horse a consul. He considered himself the equal of the gods, the brother of Jupiter, and had a temple erected to his own divinity. He dressed like a Greek god. His end came when he was assasinated in his 29th year by his own guard. He had reigned from the year 37 AD. to 41.

NERO

Nero became emperor at the age of seventeen, and reigned from 54 to 58 AD. He had excellent advisors and gave good promise, but then turned evil like Caligula. He poisoned a possible rival and had his mother put to death. He considered himself an excellent musician and people had to applaud. He also thought he was a great charioteer and, naturally, he won. He was cruel, greedy and extravagant. The rich were executed for their money. "People may hate me, if they only fear me," he said.

He had some presentiment of a changing world, but no real understanding. He wanted to participate in the destruction of the old and he set Rome on fire. The conflagration lasted for nine days and he blamed and persecuted the Christians for it. It is said that he played the fiddle while Rome burned. There was a revolt against him, but he anticipated its results by committing suicide.

The list of the famous is endless. The teacher must use his or her discretion, and not try to do too much. However, a few more names should be mentioned, if only in passing. There are the historians Livy and Tacitus; the natural scientist Pliny; the poets Virgil, Horace and Ovid; the orators and writers Cicero and Seneca.

USEFUL INFORMATION

Slavery was a regular institution of the ancient world. As far as Rome was concerned, the greater part of the slaves were prisoners of war. The masters owned them. Slaves could be bought and sold for any purpose. They could be treated cruelly or kindly. Some were chained at night. Others were trusted servants. Often there was a good relationship between master and slave. In some ways, slavery was almost like domestic service in the great houses of 18th- and 19th-century England.

When Greece was overrun, many learned Greeks were brought to Rome. They acted as scribes, artisans, tutors, educators, librarians. In the course of time, laws were made for the protection of slaves. In 200 BC, war captives were abundant and slaves had no rights. By AD 100, there was a change, and some ideas as to the rights of man were applied to slavery. Laws were enacted which at least did away with the worst abuses. A slave could not be sold to fight wild beasts; he could be paid wages as an encouragement to good service. He was given property rights, and slave marriages were recognized. It became an offense to kill or abandon slaves who were ill or unfit for work.

When a slave received payment, he could save his money and buy his freedom. Some freedmen rose to positions of importance. A master could give a slave his freedom for good service. Often, slaves were freed on the death of their master. Freedom was their legacy. Some were left fortunes.

Philosophy: The Roman mind was not a philosophical one, but practical and legalistic. Significantly, the only two systems of philosophy which appealed to the Romans were Stoicism and Epicurism, and both originated in Greece. Stoicism asserts that everything real is material. Besides matter, there is nothing but abstractions, and these have no actual existence. The Stoic praises self-control and indifference to pleasure and pain. The Epicurean philosophy is that of "eat, drink, and be merry, for tomorrow we die." The highest good obtainable is pleasure and sensual enjoyment.

From the Twelve Tables of Law, 451-452 BC

Whoever is convicted of giving false witness shall be thrown down from the Tarpeian rock.

No one shall propose to deprive a person of civil rights without a civil trial.

Any judge convicted of taking a bribe shall suffer the death penalty.

For any man whatsoever to be put to death without trial is forbidden.

From the Theodosian Code of Law

There shall be no bribery of government employees.

There shall be free access to courts and to the governor (i.e., without bribery).

Requests for bribes in civil cases shall be punishable by death.

There shall be no recognition of anonymous accusations.

From the Justinian Code

Justice is the constant, unceasing desire to render to each man his due. Contracts are obligatory in matters of purchase, sale, lease, hire, partnership, deposits, loans.

Decree of Diocletian on Inflation
Runaway inflation is so widespread that even plentiful supplies of goods are of no use in curbing it. We therefore decree maximum prices and wages. The penalty for contravening the order is death.

(There follows a price list of basic foods and drink, and wages to be paid for basic work.)

In the Markets
Market inspectors (*Aediles*) held the seller responsible for any false statement.

Working Men's Clubs
Each trade had its own club and collected subscriptions for welfare benefits. These were mainly for medical care and for the cost of the funeral. Club dinners were held. It was an offense to swear at the priest or the chairman, and fines were imposed. It was cheaper to be rude to the priest than to the chairman.

The Army
The armies of Rome were well organized. Soldiers were grouped in *centuries* (hundreds) under a Centurion. Sixty centuries made up a Legion. A soldier served for twenty years, and could then retire with a pension and a share of the booty. He was granted Roman citizenship if he did not already possess it. At first, only Romans served in the legions, but recruits from the provinces were later accepted.

Carnival Days
There were strong social classes in Rome, but these were dispensed with for a few days every year at the feast of Saturnalia. A Lord of Misrule (a mocking king) was appointed to preside over the feast. All usual work stopped. Presents were often exchanged. Prisoners were set free. Masters waited upon their slaves and guests. Masks might be worn. It was some sort of affirmation that all men are equal.

References

In the preparation of these notes, liberal reference has been made to the works of Rudolf Steiner. Since mention of history and historical characters is scattered throughout his books and lectures, it is difficult to suggest a reading list on these specific matters. For ancient history, *World History and the Mysteries in the Light of Anthroposophy* (London: Rudolf Steiner Press, 1997) would be useful. Books by Rudolf Steiner on education in general include

Essentials of Education. Hudson, New York: Anthroposophic Press, 1997.

Discussions with Teachers. Hudson, New York: Anthroposophic Press, 1997.

The Foundations of Human Experience (also translated as *Study of Man*). Hudson, New York: Anthroposophic Press, 1996.

Human Values in Education. London: Rudolf Steiner Press, 1971.

The Kingdom of Childhood.. Hudson, New York: Anthroposophic Press, 1995.

A Modern Art of Education. London: Rudolf Steiner Press, 1972.

Practical Advice to Teachers. London: Rudolf Steiner Press, 1976.

Teachers may find the following books useful. Some that are out of print may be obtainable in school or public libraries.

Bordeaux, Edmond, trans. *The Zend Avesta of Zarathustra.* San Diego, CA: Academy Books, 1973.

Brown, Norman O. *Hermes the Thief: The Evolution of a Myth.* Great Barrington, MA: Lindisfarne Press, 1990.

Bryson, Bernarda. *Gilgamesh.: Man's First Story.* Littleton, CO: Whole Spirit Press, [no date]. Also New York: Holt, Rinehart & Winston, 1967.

Buck, William. *Ramayana: King Rama's Way.* Berkeley, CA: University of California Press, 1976.

Budge, E. A. Wallis. *The Dwellers on the Nile.* New York: Dover, 1977.

Budge, E. A. Wallis. *The Gods of the Egyptians,* Vols. I and II. New York: Dover, 1969.

Colum, Padraic. *The Children's Homer: The Adventures of Odysseus and the Tale of Troy.* New York: Aladdin Paperbacks, 1918.

Colum, Padraic. *The Golden Fleece and the Heroes Who Lived before Achilles*. New York: Aladdin Paperbacks, 1921.

Coomaraswamy, Ananda K. and Sister Nivedita. *Myths of the Hindus and Buddhists*. New York: Dover, 1967.

Debusschere, Evelyn B. *The Revelation of Evolutionary Events in Myths, Stories and Legends*. Fair Oaks, CA: AWSNA, 1997.

Dryden, John, ed. *Plutarch's Lives*. New York: Dutton, 1969-1971.

Durant, Will. *The Story of Civilization*. New York: Simon & Schuster, 1954. Vol. 1, Our Oriental Heritage. Vol. 2, The Life of Greece. Vol. 3, Caesar and Christ.

Ellis, Norman. *Awakening Osiris: The Egyptian Book of the Dead*. Grand Rapids, MI: Phanes Press, 1988.

Erman, Adolf. *Life in Ancient Egypt*. New York: Dover, 1971.

Graves, Robert. *The Greek Myths*, Vols. I and II. London: Penguin Books, 1955.

Harrer, Dorothy. *Chapters from Ancient History*. Spring Valley, NY: Mercury Press, 1976.

Harrer, Dorothy. *Roman Lives*. Spring Valley, NY: Mercury Press, 1995.

Heirman, Leo. *Pictures of Initiation in Greek Mythology*. Roselle, IL: Schaumberg Publications Inc., 1987.

Hiebel, Frederick. *The Gospel of Hellas: The Mission of Ancient Greece and the Advent of Christ*. New York: Anthroposophic Press, 1949.

Kingsley, Charles. *The Heroes: Greek Fairy Tales for my Children*. New York: R.H. Russell, 1901.

Kovacs, Charles. *Ancient Mythologies: India, Persia, Babylon, Egypt*. Stourbridge, England: Wynstones Press, 1990.

Radhakrishnan, S. *The Bhagavadgita*. India: Harper Collins, 1993.

Schuré, Edouard. *From Sphinx to Christ*. Blauvelt, NY: Steinerbooks, 1970.

Schuré, Edouard. *The Great Initiates: A Study of the Secret History of Religion*. Blauvelt, NY: Steinerbooks, 1961.

Schwab, Gustav. *Gods and Heroes: Myths and Epics of Ancient Greece*. New York: Pantheon Books, 1946.

Seeger, Elizabeth. *The Five Sons of King Pandu: The Story of the Mahabharata*. New York: William R. Scott, 1967.

Spence, Lewis. *Ancient Egyptian Myths and Legends*. New York: Dover, 1990.

About the Author

Roy Wilkinson has been connected with the work of Rudolf Steiner for over 60 years. Born in Leicestershire, England, he was educated both locally and in Switzerland. He attended the Goetheanum School of Speech and Drama, receiving his certificate from Frau Dr. Steiner herself.

Afte working at an educational center, he made excursions int ... fields of medicine (with Weleda) and agriculture, and eventually became a teacher. Over some forty years he taught in Steiner and State schools in England, Germany, and Switzerland. He has also taught children in need of special care.

Mr. Wilkinson has been active as an advisor to schools and lecturer on Rudolf Steiner education and Anthroposophy in many European countries, in South America as well as in English-speaking countries.

Another major contribution is the writing he has done over a period of more than twenty years. Wilkinson has produced introductory books on Rudolf Steiner education and its philosophical foundations. These and his curriculum guide booklets have been highly appreciated by teachers, parents, and those seeking answers to personal questions. A complete list of current editions is at the end of this volume.

BOOKS BY ROY WILKINSON

Questions and Answers on Rudolf Steiner Education
The Temperaments in Education
The Interpretation of Fairy Tales
The Curriculum of the Rudolf Steiner School
Commonsense Schooling

Wilkinson Waldorf Curriculum Series:

Teaching English
Teaching Mathematics
Teaching Physics and Chemistry
Teaching Geography
Teaching History I: *Ancient Civilizations, Greece, Rome*
Teaching History II: *Middle Ages, Renaissance to Second World War*
Old Testament Stories
Commentary on the Old Testament Stories
The Norse Stories and Their Significance
Teaching Practical Activities: *Farming, Gardening, Housebuilding*
The Human Being and the Animal World
Plant Study and Geology
Nutrition, Health, and Anthropology
Miscellany: *A Collection of Poems and Plays*
Plays for Puppets

The Origin and Development of Language
The Spiritual Basis of Rudolf Steiner Education

Rudolf Steiner: Aspects of his spiritual world view (3 volumes)

Anthroposophy vol. I: *Rudolf Steiner. Reincarnation and karma. The Spiritual Nature of the human being. The development of human consciousness.*

Anthroposophy vol. II: *Evolution of the world and humanity. Relationships between the living and the dead. Forces of evil. The modern path of initiation.*

Anthroposophy vol. III: *Life between death and rebirth. The spiritual hierarchies. The philosophical approach to the spirit. The mission of Christ.*

May be Ordered from: Rudolf Steiner College Bookstore
9200 Fair Oaks Boulevard
Fair Oaks, CA 95628, USA
Tel: (916) 961-8729 — Fax: (916) 961-3032